The Lutheran Handbook II

About "Winking Luther(s)"

Martin Luther's theology is grounded in paradoxes—sinner/saint, law/gospel, hidden/revealed—and illuminated by a down-to-earth, everyday sense of humor. This icon of Luther winking at the reader combines the serious, formal scholarship that was his life's work with the humor and lightheartedness that characterized his personality.

The wink on Luther's face indicates that even though theology is serious stuff, we should nonetheless remember that it is not our theology that saves us, but Jesus Christ. Therefore, our life in the church can be buoyant, and our theological wranglings can be done with a sense of humor and love for our neighbor.

Because this second book, *The Lutheran Handbook II*, takes after its predecessor, *The Lutheran Handbook*, in almost every way, it is logical that "Winking Luther" should appear on the cover once again. Since it is a sequel of sorts, however, with 100 percent new content delivered in exactly the same style, a single "Winkie" would not do. Therefore, two identical Winking Luthers appear on the cover to communicate to you, dear reader, that the volume you hold in your hands is both twice as good and twice as important as the first handbook was.

The Lutheran Handbook II

Augsburg Fortress

Minneapolis

THE LUTHERAN HANDBOOK II

Elements of Worst-Case Scenario Survival Handbook® trade dress have been used with permission of and under license from Quirk Productions, Inc. Based on the trade dress of The Worst-Case Scenario Survival Handbook Series, by Joshua Piven and David Borgenicht, published by Chronicle Books, LLC. Worst-Case Scenario ® and The Worst-Case Scenario Survival Handbook® are registered trademarks of Quirk Productions, Inc., 215 Church Street, Philadelphia, PA 19106.

Scripture quotations are from the New Revised Standard Version Bible, copyright © 1989, Division of Christian Education of the National Council of the Churches of Christ in the United States of America. Used by permission. All rights reserved.

Pages 202 and 253: Quotations from *Luther's Works*, vol. 14, copyright © 1958 Concordia Publishing House, and vol. 35, copyright © 1960 Fortress Press.

Page 38: The Rev. James Jones quote is from a Jan. 29, 2006, interview "God's Grace," on *Songs of Praise*, a BBC radio program.

Pages 122-133: Glossary reprinted from *Altar Guild and Sacristy Handbook*, by S. Anita Stauffer, copyright © 2000 Augsburg Fortress.

Pages 280-296: Translation of Luther's Small Catechism from *The Book of Concord*, Robert Kolb and Timothy J. Wengert, eds. © 2000 Augsburg Fortress. All rights reserved. This altered version is from *Evangelical Lutheran Worship*.

New brand development editor: Kristofer Skrade
Editors: Barbara S. Wilson and Arlene Flancher
Production editors: Linnea Fitzpatrick, James Satter, Eileen Engebretson, and Josh Messner
Interior illustrator: Brenda Brown

Contributing writers: Rod Anderson, Chip Borgstadt, Ramona S. Bouzard, Walter C. Bouzard, Eric Burtness, Louis R. Carlozo, Carol Carver, Chris Duckworth, Rod Hank, Paul N. Hanson, Susan Houglum, Mark J. Jackson, Rolf A. Jacobson, Mark D. Johns, Mark K. Johnson, Ken Sundet Jones, James Kasperson, Timothy Keyl, Charles R. Lane, Susan M. Lang, Catherine Malotky, Mark C. Mattes, Sally Messner, Jennifer Moland-Kovash, Seth Moland-Kovash, Paul Owens, Rebecca Ninke, Marc Ostlie-Olson, Tom Teichmann, Megan J. Thorvilson, Megan Torgerson, Erik Ullestad, Darin Wiebe, Hans Wiersma, and Steven Zittergruen

ISBN 978-0-8066-7037-9

The paper used in this publication meets the minimum requirements of American National Standard for Information Sciences—Permanence of Paper for Printed Library Materials, ANSI Z329.48-1984.

Manufactured in the U.S.A.

11   10   09   08   07   2   3   4   5   6   7   8   9   10

CONTENTS

This Book Belongs To	10
About My Congregation	11
Preface	12

Church Stuff

15

How to Identify the True Christian Church on Earth	16
Ten Key Leaders of the Early Christian Church	19
Ten Important Lutheran Events since the Reformation	22
The Lutheran Reformers' Five Most Dastardly Theological Opponents	26
The Most Outrageous Luther Quotes and What They Mean	29
Top Five Lutheran Myths and Why We Choose Not to Debunk Them	32
Five Important Reformers Other than Martin Luther	35
Luther's Germany	39
Ten Important Lutherans since the Reformation and What They Did	42
Five Great Lutheran Composers and What They Wrote	46
Five Famous Lutheran Artists and What They Made	49
Top Five Contributions by Women of the Church	51
Seven Important Lutheran Missionaries and Where They Went	54
A Brief History of the Lutheran Choral Tradition	56
How to Identify a Traditional Worship Devotee	59
How to Identify a Contemporary Worship Devotee	62

How to Usher   65

How to Acolyte   68

How to Be a Greeter   72

Five Common Worship Practices and Why
    Lutherans Do Them   75

How to Read Scripture Aloud during Worship   77

How to Chant   81

How to Set the Communion Table   84

How to Assist during Communion Distribution   88

How to Deliver Communion to a Homebound Person   91

How to Deliver a Temple Talk/Make an Announcement
    during Worship   94

Important Institutions Every Lutheran Should
    Know About   96

The Lutheran Family Tree   98

A Brief History of the Lutheran Movement   102

Common Types of Lutheran Clergy Garb   106

Names for Lutheran Worship Furnishings, Ministers,
    Paraments, and Vestments   108

Lutheran Denominations in North America   110

Lutheran Colleges and Universities in North America   114

ELCA Congregations in the United States   120

Glossary of Lutheran Worship Terms   122

Everyday Stuff 135

How to Receive God's Grace Daily 136

How to Proclaim the Gospel to Someone
Who Needs to Hear It 139

The Top Three Uses of the Law 142

How to Heap Grace on Your Enemies' Heads Like Hot Coals 145

How to Tell the Difference between Cheap Grace and
Regular Grace 148

How to Repent 151

How to Identify a "Neighbor" and What This Means
for Lutherans 153

How to Adopt an Evangelistic Lifestyle without Alienating
People 155

How to Tithe 158

Seven Complicated Lutheran Theological Terms in Latin
and What They Mean in Plain English 161

How to Tell the Difference between a "Vocation" and
a "Vacation" 164

How to Tell the Difference between Justice and Charity 168

How to Tell the Difference between Theology of the Cross
and Theology of Glory 170

How to Tell the Difference between the Kingdom on the Left
and the Kingdom on the Right 174

How to Tell If Your Will Is in Bondage to Sin and What
to Do about It 178

How to Tell the Difference between a Lutheran Pietist and
a Lutheran Confessionalist 181

How to Tell the Difference between Original Sin and
Everyday Sin 184

How to Tell the Difference between a Sinner and a Saint 186

How to Tell the Difference between a Lutheran Conservative
and a Lutheran Liberal   188

The Four Most Common Heresies Well-Intentioned
Lutherans Commit   191

How to Show the World You're a Lutheran without Being
Flashy or Boring   193

How to Handle Yourself When You Get Angry at God   196

How to Invite a Friend or Neighbor to Church without
Terrifying Them   198

How to Memorize Luther's Small Catechism   202

Bible Stuff   207

A Brief History of the Bible   208

How to Choose a Bible Translation That's Right for You   212

How to Read the Entire Bible in One Year   215

How to Start a Bible Study Group   218

The Five Grossest Bible Diseases   221

Top Five Scary Monsters in the Bible   223

Top Seven Dastardly Bible Deeds   226

Top Seven Acts of Human Kindness in the Bible   229

Top Five Sibling Rivalries in the Bible   232

Top 10 Angel Sightings in the Bible   234

Five Most Common Images for God in the Bible   237

Top Five "Other Gods" in the Old Testament and
Who Believed in Them   239

How to Identify an Angel   241

The Five Most Unpopular Old Testament Prophets   244

Five Inspiring Women in the Bible   246

Top Five Misconceptions about the Book of Revelation   248

How to Tell When the Apocalypse Is Imminent   250

How to Locate the "Canon within the Canon"   252

How to Listen to Scripture as it is Read Aloud and
Get Something Out of It   254

Seven Important Bible Teachings Every Lutheran
Should Know   256

Ten Common Occupations in Bible Times   258

Top 10 Prayers Uttered in the Bible   262

Top 10 Curses Uttered in the Bible   265

A Brief History of God's Covenant with the People   268

How to Read Key Types of Bible Literature: 270

- A Psalm
- A Prophetic Message
- A Parable
- A Letter
- A Narrative Account
- A Proverb

How to Interpret "Controversial" Bible Texts and
Remain Lutheran   275

Small Catechism of Martin Luther   279

Notes & Stuff   297

This Book Belongs To

Name _____

Address _____

_____

E-mail _____

Telephone _____

Birth date _____

Baptismal birth date _____

First communion _____

Confirmation date _____

Godparents' (baptismal sponsors') names

_____

_____

_____

_____

Churches I've belonged to:	*Years of membership*
_____	_____
_____	_____
_____	_____
_____	_____
_____	_____
_____	_____

✠

About My Congregation

Name _____

Address_____

_____

Year organized/founded _____

My pastor(s) _____

_____

_____

_____

Number of baptized members_____

Average weekly worship attendance _____

Facts about my denomination _____

_____

_____

_____

Other information about my congregation and faith

_____

_____

_____

_____

✠

PREFACE

If you thought *The Lutheran Handbook* (Augsburg Fortress, 2005) was a good guide to Lutheran church culture but have fondly dreamt of a similar guide to the world of higher Lutheran theology and Lutheran church history, your dreams have been answered. *The Lutheran Handbook II* is even more Lutheran than the first one was, and it still has all the practical, down-to-earth, step-by-step helps for navigating your way along the path.

Why did we publish the handbook on church culture first and the theology one second, you may ask? Because poking fun at Lutheran church culture is easy—every confirmand, pastor, and church council member in the world does it—and making Lutheran theology fun, funny, clear, and accessible is more difficult, that's why. (It should be underlined, here, that we are *not* attempting in this book to make fun of Martin Luther, the Lutheran reformers, Lutheran theology, or the treasured doctrinal heritage and biblical insight that make Lutherans Lutheran. Actual living Lutherans themselves, however, are fair game.) You, dear reader, must be the judge of whether we have accomplished our task or not.

Getting Lutheran theology "right" while simultaneously revealing the brilliant humor and liberating lightness of being that it can elicit proves a truly elusive goal. In *The Lutheran Handbook II* we may have erred in some cases on the side of clearer concepts at the expense of humor and in other cases just the reverse. Such error is in some sense unavoidable. The point is that we strove overall to strike a balance between the two, humor and substance, so that a more accurate and complete picture of the whole can come to light. In other words, try and keep a sense of humor while you read, okay?

We should disclaim at this point that any bad theology, offense, crises of faith, affliction of the conscience, mal-adjustment, or cognitive dissonance arising from the reading of this book is purely the responsibility of the reader. On the other hand, any enlightenment, clarity, insight, renewal, reform, maturation, growth, or truth arising from the reading of this book may be directly attributed to the editors. We encourage you to use this book for the purposes of learning, teaching, and conversation and not in the contravention of any municipal, state, or federal laws or statutes. The publisher is not responsible for any physical injury resulting from reading this book, either, though such a scenario is difficult to imagine, especially among Lutherans.

—THE EDITORS

CHURCH STUFF

HOW TO IDENTIFY THE TRUE CHRISTIAN CHURCH ON EARTH

As Martin Luther himself once asked, "How will or how can a poor, confused person tell where such Christian, holy people are to be found in this world?" The key is not to focus on the people themselves, since human beings are pretty unreliable, but on what God is doing that brings the people together.

Where the Word is preached to sinners and the sacraments are given, that is the church on earth. Outside of that it's kind of iffy.

❶ Employ a simple, straightforward definition; keep it clear.

Article 7 of the Augsburg Confession* claims that the one, holy, Christian Church "is the assembly of all believers among whom the gospel is rightly preached and the holy sacraments are administered according to the gospel." Uncluttered is better.

❷ Actively embrace the unorthodox orthodoxy of the Lutheran definition.

Lutherans propose a somewhat radical understanding of "church." Believers are organized around the purely preached Word and the giving of the sacraments rather than under popes and bishops. In fact, Luther and other reformers were quite harsh in their criticism of popes and bishops who did *not* support the pure preaching of the gospel.

❸ Consider a broader definition only when absolutely necessary.

Lutherans identify seven visible signs of the "One, True Church on Earth": (1) The Word of God, (2) Holy Baptism, (3) Holy Communion, (4) The Forgiveness of Sin (and the Admonition against it), (5) The Office of the Ministry, (6) Worship, and (7) The Cross, that is, persecution for the sake of gospel.

---

* The Augsburg Confession is the primary confession of faith of the Lutheran church and one of its most important documents.

❹ If all else fails, listen for the gospel and look for the sacraments.
Where and when God bestows grace and salvation through Jesus Christ proclaimed and the sacraments, that is the church. You can only be sure of the church's presence where these things happen. Outside of that it's kind of iffy.

Be Aware

- Lutherans believe that the Church is hidden in Christ until the day Christ himself is revealed in glory. When Jesus comes to judge the living and dead, only then will the true assembly be revealed. Therefore, Christians who think they can say who is *in and who is not* in the body of Christ should be viewed with suspicion.
- In 1521, Martin Luther's excommunication from the Roman church became official. It should not come as a surprise, therefore, that Lutheran Christians adhere to a different concept of "the True Christian Church on Earth" than, say, Roman Catholic Christians, even though we get along with them really well nowadays.
- Despite the sharp disagreements Lutherans had with the Roman church, they were originally willing to allow the authority of the pope—if only the pope would allow the Lutheran preaching of the gospel. That didn't work out so well.
- God gathers the church to hear the gospel and receive the sacraments, but these gifts are for sinners only. Non-sinners need not apply.

TEN KEY LEADERS OF THE EARLY CHRISTIAN CHURCH

Among many Lutherans, the first ancestors of the Christian movement receive too little press, often in favor of our particular ancestors from the Reformation. Here is but a very small sampling.

 Peter (? –ca. 64).
Jesus says of his disciple Peter (Matthew 16:18), "On this rock I will build my church." This prophesy is partially realized when Peter preaches following the formation of the Church (Acts 2). Peter is a leader of the earliest Christians in Jerusalem.

 Paul (ca. 10–ca. 65).
As a faithful Jew, Saul participated in the persecution of Christians before Jesus called him to become an apostle. As Paul, he then devoted his life to traveling and spreading the gospel. The letters he wrote to churches became the earliest-written books of the New Testament.

❸ Origen (185–ca. 254).
One of the most brilliant early Christians, Origen spent his life teaching and writing. Origen lived in a spiritually disciplined manner and is considered one of spiritual fathers of monastic life.

❹ Perpetua (ca. 199–ca. 203, as late as 211).
This new Christian was persecuted and killed for her beliefs. Perpetua is representative of the thousands of early Christians who accepted death before renouncing Christ.

Perpetua and Felicitas were key leaders of the early Christian church through their extraordinary witness to Jesus in defiance of the civil authorities, which brought about their martyrdom. Perpetua authored the earliest Christian writings by a woman.

❺ Lawrence (225–258).
An early church deacon, he is most famous for the story of his death. Ordered to turn over the church's treasures, he presented the needy as the true treasures of the church instead. As punishment he was to be slowly burnt to death over a fire where, after a time, he bravely said, "I am done on this side, turn me over!"

⑥ Emperor Constantine (272–337).
This Roman emperor converted to Christianity, ostensibly after a religious experience in battle. As the religion became favored by the Roman Empire, the early church quickly swelled in both numbers and influence.

⑦ Athanasius (ca. 293–373).
A gifted scholar and church leader, Athanasius argued against false doctrine his whole life. Against his own will, he was made a bishop in his later years.

⑧ John Chrysostom (349–407).
Chrysostom was the bishop of the city of Constantinople. He preached and spoke powerfully and was a gifted theologian. He is responsible for culling many of the elements of modern Christian worship from Scripture.

⑨ Jerome (ca. 347–420).
His fiery temper and brilliant mind drove Jerome throughout his life. He is primarily known for his translation of the entire Bible into Latin. His translation came to be used by most of Christendom for more than 1,000 years.

⑩ Augustine (354–430).
Although born in a little town in North Africa to unimportant parents, Augustine became one of the most influential people the Church has ever known; a scholar, a teacher, a bishop, and a writer whose works have influenced theologians for centuries.

TEN IMPORTANT LUTHERAN EVENTS SINCE THE REFORMATION

Not every important event in Lutheran history happened between 1517 and 1546 (the period of the Reformation). The Lutheran church is a living tradition that has been carried on by faithful sinners for five centuries.

1 The Peace of Augsburg (1555).
This agreement helped stop the armed conflict between German evangelical princes and their opponents in the Roman church and Empire. It gave those princes permission to choose how Christianity should be taught and practiced in their territories. (See also item 9 below.)

After Martin Luther's death, his friends and colleagues still had a lot of difficult issues to resolve. Their written resolutions were eventually published as The Book of Concord, *which is quite thick and heavy.*

❷ *The Book of Concord* (1580).

After Luther's death, his followers struggled with questions that threatened to split the evangelical movement. Fifty years after the presentation of the Augsburg Confession, they drafted a solution to those questions and pointed to other writings that defined what they believed. This Formula of Concord and those writings were published as *The Book of Concord* and form the core of Lutheran teaching and shape its preaching.

❸ Bartholomäus Ziegenbalg and Heinrich Plütschau (1705).

King Frederick IV of Denmark commissioned these two German pastors as the first Lutheran missionaries to spread the gospel outside of Europe. They went to preach in India and launched Lutheranism into the wider world.

❹ The Prussian Union's New Church (1830).

King Frederick William III of Prussia wanted to create a united Protestant church from two branches that had been at odds since the Reformation: the followers of Luther and those of Calvin. Many individuals liked the visible unity, but a large number of "old Lutherans" rejected it. As a result, there was a revival in studying the Lutheran Confessions.

❺ Lutheran Europeans emigrate (18th through 20th centuries).

Europeans from historically Lutheran lands like Germany and Scandinavia immigrated to North America, South America, and Australia. These Lutherans started congregations, trained pastors, and established schools, laying the foundation of Lutheran teaching and preaching in those places and around the world today.

❻ The Luther Renaissance (1883 to the present).
At the end of the 19th century, the new Weimar edition of *Luther's Works* was published and allowed historians and pastors to read what Luther actually said. It sparked the Luther Renaissance, a scholarly explosion in which a new, fuller image of Luther began to emerge. More than a luminary and scholar, Luther was also a down-to-earth pastor, husband, colleague, father, and friend deeply involved in the nitty-gritty of life.

❼ The Barmen Declaration (1934).
Many Christians under Adolf Hitler's regime went along with the Nazis' use of Luther and Christianity to justify and support their actions. Members of the Confessing Church, including Lutherans, composed the Barmen Declaration to oppose Hitler and call their Christian brothers and sisters back to faith. Led by the Reformed theologian Karl Barth, they opposed the church's compromises with the Nazi party.

❽ The Lutheran World Federation (1947).
The Lutheran World Federation (LWF) was established to help coordinate the mission of the churches that have arisen in the original Lutheran territories and in all those places where missionaries and European emigrants brought the good news of Christ. LWF represents 66 million Lutherans and especially assists Lutheran churches in the developing world.

⑨ Lutherans and Catholics (1999).
Since Luther's excommunication in the 16th century, Lutherans and Roman Catholics have been split on doctrine and practice. The *Joint Declaration on the Doctrine of Justification* between member churches of the LWF and the Roman Catholic Church sought to bring the parties together by describing a common understanding of the gospel.

⑩ Your life's work (right now).
"Jesus Christ died for you and claims you as his own." Just as it does in your baptism and the Lord's Supper, this gospel message has just now, as you read it, entered into the grave of your sin to give you faith and raise you from the dead. (Pass it on!) Mark this page and come back to watch Lutheran history as it happens again and again. The days of your life *are* the unfolding future of the Lutheran tradition.

Be Aware

- The Holy Spirit still guides the Lutheran church, though we seem fully capable of messing things up on our own from time to time.
- Lutherans are always reforming the church because that's how the Spirit works.
- The church is a living, dynamic organism where the Spirit finds new ways to lead and guide sinners into truth.

THE LUTHERAN REFORMERS' FIVE MOST DASTARDLY THEOLOGICAL OPPONENTS

1 Erasmus of Rotterdam.

Luther and Erasmus engaged in a heated battle over the idea of "free will." When Erasmus said we need specialists to explain a confusing and contradictory Bible, Luther said the problem was his belief in free will. If we understand our bondage to sin, then Scripture is perfectly clear: It's the story of God's work to compel sinners to faith.

Erasmus of Rotterdam was one of the Lutheran reformers' most dastardly theological opponents. He opposed Luther over the idea of free will.

❷ Johann Eck.

Eck was one of Luther's earliest foes. He claimed that Luther was a heretic who upset the church's order and encouraged people to rebel. In short, the Christian freedom Luther preached was a threat to the church and society. Luther responded with the Heidelberg Disputation, a presentation to his fellow Augustinian monks about the core of his teaching, and later with treatises like *On the Freedom of a Christian.*

❸ Andreas Carlstadt.

Carlstadt had been Luther's colleague at the University of Wittenberg but became a firebrand who never thought Luther went far enough. Luther saw Carlstadt as one of the so-called *Schwärmer,* the frantic, buzzing enthusiasts who always wanted something extra to go with God's serving of grace in Christ Jesus: a certain feeling, a direct revelation, or a moral rejuvenation. Luther countered that God's promise was enough.

❹ Johann Agricola.

Agricola had been one of Luther's favorite students but turned against his teacher over the question of the law. Agricola argued that Christians are completely freed from God's demand to do good works. For Luther, that could be true if the new faithful person in us were all that we are. But since we're always simultaneously justified and sinful, we need the law preached to us until our dying breath.

⑤ The hidden God.
Any time Luther tried to find God apart from what has been revealed in Christ, terror was the only result. How could he ever know if he'd ever done enough to please God and merit salvation? The more he tried to find the hidden God, the more he understood the gravity of his situation. The question hounded him his entire life, but he always found consolation in God's promise: Jesus had died for a sinner such as him.

Be Aware

- Although four of the five opponents are dead, the issues they raised are alive and well. Luther's response to each remains the best one possible: Preach Christ's justification for the sake of sinners.

THE MOST OUTRAGEOUS LUTHER QUOTES AND WHAT THEY MEAN

❶ "A 'god' is the thing we look to for all good and where we try to find refuge when we're in need." *(The Large Catechism)*
The thing in your life you most trust or fear losing is your god. It can be your health, status, control, or continuing existence, among other things. All statements about sin revolve around whom you ultimately trust. God wants to be that one.

❷ "Sin boldly." *(Letter to Philip Melanchthon)*
Christianity isn't for good people. It's for sinners. So Luther encouraged people to fess up to their sinfulness and then trust even more in Christ's mercy. (See page 149 for a complete quote.)

❸ "The Jews are actually closer to Christ than we are." *(That Jesus Christ Was Born a Jew)*
In contrast to his often quoted words against the Jews, Luther argued here that we ought to respect Jewish people as chosen by God and regard ourselves as adopted into the family through Christ's death and resurrection.

❹ "The human will is placed between God and the Devil like a beast of burden." *(Bondage of the Will)*
Free will is an illusion. Our will is controlled either by God or the devil. God takes the reins whenever the Word brings faith.

❺ "A theologian of the cross teaches that punishments, crosses, and death are the most precious savings account of all." *(Explanations of the Ninety-five Theses)*
Salvation is best encountered in places where God first seems absent, rather than in power, success, and glory. That's where our cross is joined to Christ's.

❻ "When you have faith you have to stick with Christ incarnate in the manger. If you want to climb higher and take a look at our Lord God's work, you'll fall." *(Commentary on Isaiah 66:1)*
God reveals God's self in Christ Jesus, and that's where we ought to look. Without him, you'll never find anything but terror or a mirror image of yourself.

❼ "I stomp all over reason and its wisdom and say, 'Shut up, you cursed whore! Are you trying to seduce me into committing fornication with the devil?'" *(The Last Sermon in Wittenberg)*
Theology that serves as its own end does no one any good and ought to be condemned. But theology that serves to preach the gospel in its truth and purity is theology properly done.

❽ "Good, modest churches with low arches are the best for preachers and for listeners, for the ultimate reason for these buildings isn't the bellowing and bawling of choir members but the Word of God and its proclamation." *(Table Talk, 3781)*
A sanctuary right out of *Better Divine Homes and Churches* may be nice to look at, but if the law and gospel aren't heard there it's missing the point. A good sound system beats beautiful architecture hands down.

9 "Women and maidens have started baring themselves in front and back, and there isn't anyone who punishes or objects." *(Letter to Katie Luther, 1545)*
Things were never this bad in my day. What is this generation coming to?

10 "I don't know any other comfort, help, or counsel for my salvation except that Christ is my mercy seat." *(Sermon on the Sum of the Christian Life)*
Sinners always want to look for something other than Christ to bring them salvation. But Luther proclaims that Christ's mercy is more than enough—it's everything.

Luther asserted that churches with low arches are best because they facilitate the preaching and hearing of God's word.

TOP FIVE LUTHERAN MYTHS AND WHY WE CHOOSE NOT TO DEBUNK THEM

Myths are notions that help hold a culture together. Just as Americans have upheld legends about their heroes, like "George Washington had wooden teeth" (they were actually made of gold and ivory) and proclaimed, "I cannot tell a lie," when his father confronted him (never happened), Lutherans have done the same with Martin Luther. Here are the top five Lutheran myths and why they survive.

❶ Luther nailed his Ninety-five Theses to the church door in order to take on the powerful Roman Catholic Church.
The only surviving report that Luther posted the Ninety-five Theses to the door of the castle chapel in Wittenberg comes from Luther's friend Philip Melanchthon. In those days church doors doubled as public bulletin boards. The Ninety-five Theses begin with a public service announcement of sorts: "The following theses will be publicly discussed at Wittenberg under the chairmanship of the reverend father Martin Luther." While there is reason to believe Melanchthon's report, Luther didn't post the Ninety-five Theses in order to challenge the powers that be to a fight. Instead, he merely did what many teachers still do: provide a discussion guide. We keep this one going because we like David-and-Goliath stories.

❷ **Luther defied pope and emperor with the words, "Here I stand; I can do no other!"**
The words "Here I stand" are not included in the original written reports. At the Diet of Worms in 1521, Luther was asked if he would renounce his controversial writings. Luther's defiant statement ended with these words: "I cannot and I will not recant anything for to go against conscience is neither right nor safe. God help me. Amen." Defiant, perhaps, but not quite as dramatic.

❸ **Luther never intended to start his own church.**
This one's kind of true. At first Luther hoped to reform the Roman church while remaining a faithful member of it. Emphasizing Luther's (original) faithfulness helps facilitate ecumenical dialogue. But the fact is the pope excommunicated Luther in 1520. As the years wore on and as the chance for reconciliation with Rome became more and more remote, Luther and other reformers began to train clergy and organize congregations without the blessing of the Roman church. At that point Luther focused on keeping the gospel alive by creating and supporting new mechanisms and structures.

❹ **Luther invented the Christmas tree.**
The story goes that Luther was walking through the woods one Christmas night. He marveled at the way the stars shimmered through the pine branches. When he came home, he wanted to show his children what he'd seen. So he cut down a tree, brought it inside, and stuck candles in it. This legend is just one more example of how Christians have "baptized" pagan holidays—in this case the winter solstice feast.

⑤ Luther threw an inkwell at the devil.
Luther once wrote that he threw ink at the devil, but this was a metaphorical reference to his translating the New Testament into German. The metaphor means that the ink of Luther's own writing—and via the printing press—to bring the Bible into people's lives was a boon to faith and a bane to Satan. At some point, however, the statement began to be interpreted literally. As a result, the myth arose that while Luther was tortured by his situation in exile and beset by doubts, the devil visited him in Wartburg Castle. Then Luther threw an inkwell at the devil to chase him away. This myth morphed into yet another in which the inkwell was actually a full chamber pot, which is more dramatic and much grosser.

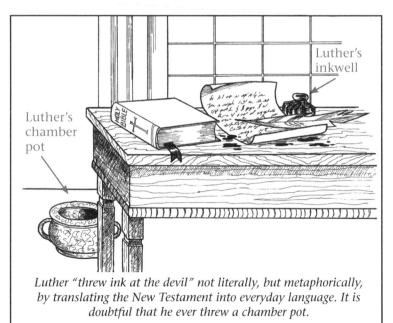

Luther "threw ink at the devil" not literally, but metaphorically, by translating the New Testament into everyday language. It is doubtful that he ever threw a chamber pot.

FIVE IMPORTANT REFORMERS OTHER THAN MARTIN LUTHER

Many people make the mistake of believing Luther was the only person working for church reform during the tumultuous 16th century. In fact, there were many important reformers. Some of them were quite famous, in fact, though many had theological quarrels with Luther. Here are just five of them.

❶ Desiderius Erasmus (1466?–1536).
- Spoke out against church corruption, including the sale of indulgences.
- Wrote the best-seller *The Praise of Folly* (1511), which lampooned the clergy and Christian superstition.
- Emphasized the "Philosophy of Christ" and reading Greek and Latin classics.
- Influenced many later reformers deeply, including Bucer and Melanchthon.
- Opposed Luther on several key reforms, especially in the famous debate regarding the "Freedom of the Will."
- a.k.a. Erasmus of Rotterdam, he never married.

❷ Ulrich Zwingli (1484–1531).
- Led the Swiss Reformation, bringing reform to Zürich and the region.
- Held that baptism was, in part, a human pledge to "amend" one's life for good.
- Did not tolerate musical instruments in worship.
- Quarreled with Luther regarding the nature of Christ's presence in the Lord's Supper.
- Lived with and eventually married Anna Reinhard.
- Died in battle while defending a Swiss town from an anti-Reform army during a surprise attack.

❸ Martin Bucer (1491–1551).
- Led reforming efforts in southern German towns and cities (especially Strasburg).
- Was present at the Diet of Worms; converted to Luther's views thereafter.
- Was present at Marburg, mediating the discussion between Zwingli and Luther.
- Pursued agreement with Lutherans regarding the Lord's Supper; signed the *Wittenberg Concord* (1536) as a result.
- Corresponded with and befriended many key reformers, including everybody else named in this list.
- One of the first priests to marry, in 1521 he wed a former nun, Elizabeth Silbereisen, and was excommunicated for it.

❹ Philipp Melanchthon (1497–1560).
- Entered the University of Heidelberg at age 12 and published an edition of a Greek classic at age 18.
- Joined the Wittenberg faculty in 1518 as a professor of biblical languages.
- Wrote a theological textbook (*Loci Communes*) in 1522 at the age of 25.
- Penned two central Lutheran documents: the *Augsburg Confession* and the *Apology to the Augsburg Confession*.
- After Luther's death in 1546, led the Wittenberg reform movement through difficult political times.
- In 1520, married the unfortunately named Katherina Krapp. But she was the daughter of Wittenberg's mayor so nobody laughed.

Philipp Melanchthon, though homely, was a profound influence on the Lutheran reformation and contributed greatly to its most important writings.

⑤ John Calvin (1509–1564).

- Originally a lawyer, became a reformer during the 1530s, after what he called a "sudden conversion."
- Wrote the influential *Institutes of the Christian Religion*, first published in 1536.
- Led the reformation of Geneva, Switzerland, where Calvin's rule enjoyed political force.
- Enjoyed cordial correspondence with Melanchthon, especially after Luther's death.
- His reforming efforts eventually held sway in Switzerland, northern France, the Netherlands, and Scotland.
- In 1539, married Idelette de Bure, a widow with two children.

Be Aware

- These are only five of the many different people who helped reform Christian doctrine and practice during the 16th century, and splintered the unity of the Roman church in the process!
- Honorable mentions include William Tyndale, Thomas More, Jacob Hutter, Ignatius Loyola, and Katharina von Bora, who helped reform the Christian household.

LUTHER'S GERMANY

1483 Martin Luther is born on November 10 in Eisleben, Germany. He is the son of Hans and Margarethe Luther.

1488–1497 Young Martin attends school in Mansfeld.

1497–1498 He attends school in Magdeburg.

1498–1501 He attends school in Eisenach.

1501–1505 Martin Luther studies at Erfurt University and graduates with an M.A. degree (master of the seven liberal arts). At his father's request, he switches to jurisprudence.

1505 On July 2, Luther is overtaken by a thunderstorm near Stotternheim. When lightning strikes nearby, he vows to become a monk. On July 17, he enters the Monastery of the Augustinian Mendicant Friars in Erfurt.

1507 Luther is ordained as a priest.

1508-1510 He lectures on philosophy and theology in Wittenberg and Erfurt.

1510/1511 He travels to Rome on matters concerning the Augustinian Order.

1512 Luther becomes professor of theology and lecturer in interpretation of the Scriptures at Wittenberg University. From 1513–1518, he gives important lectures on the book of Psalms and the letters to Romans, Galatians, and Hebrews.

1517 On October 31, Luther nails his Ninety-five Theses denouncing the dispensation of indulgences to the door of the palace church in Wittenberg.

1518 On October 12-14, he is interrogated by Cardinal Cajetan in Augsburg.

1519   In June and July, the disputation with Eck in Leipzig, during which time Luther challenges the pope's infallibility.

1520/1521   Three of Luther's major works on the Reformation are published: "To the Christian Nobility of the German Nation," "On the Freedom of a Christian Person," and "On the Babylonian Captivity of the Church."

1520   Luther burns the Canon Law and the Papal bull of condemnation in front of the Elster Gate in Wittenberg.

1521	On January 3, Luther is excommunicated by the pope. On April 17-18, Luther defends himself before the Imperial Diet in Worms. He refuses to recant, as demanded by the Emperor Karl V, and is banned by him.
1521–1522	Luther is rescued by the Elector Frederick the Wise and taken to the Wartburg where, disguised as Junker Jörg, he translates the New Testament.
1522	Luther returns to Wittenberg.
1525	Nürnberg becomes the first imperial town to adopt the Reformation. That year, Martin Luther marries a former nun, Katharina von Bora. They have three sons and three daughters in the years that follow.
1529	By this time, Luther finishes compiling the Large and Small Catechisms.
1530	Martin Luther, Philip Melanchthon, Justus Jonas, and Johannes Bugenhagen compile the Torgau Articles, which form the basis of the Augsburg Confession. Luther stays in Coburg Fortress during the Imperial Diet in Augsburg.
1534	Luther's translation of the entire Old and New Testaments appears in print.
1537	In Schmalkalden, at the instigation of the Elector Frederick the Magnanimous, Luther compiles the "Schmalkalden Articles" (the main elements of the advice proffered to the league of Protestant towns and princes).
1544	The consecration by Luther of the palace church in Torgau, the first Protestant ecclesiatical building.
1545/1546	Luther pays three visits to his original home in order to settle legal disputes between the counts of Mansfeld.
1546	Martin Luther dies in Eisleben on February 18. He is buried in the palace church in Wittenberg on February 22.

TEN IMPORTANT LUTHERANS SINCE THE REFORMATION AND WHAT THEY DID

1 Henry Melchior Mühlenberg (1711–1787).
A German pastor who responded to the call by Lutherans in North America for trained clergy, he moved to Philadelphia in 1742 and organized congregations throughout the area in the Ministerium of Pennsylvania, the first Lutheran synod (cooperative group) in North America in 1748.

2 C. F. W. Walther (1811–1887).
Walther took over the leadership of a group of Lutheran immigrants in Missouri after their first leader was dismissed. Walther was the first president of The Lutheran Church—Missouri Synod, seminary professor, seminary president, and founder and editor of a theological journal and a newspaper. He was also a prolific author and parish pastor.

3 Paul Tillich (1886–1965).
Tillich was ordained in 1912 and taught in universities throughout Germany. He was fired in 1933 for his refusal to join the Nazi Party. He immigrated to New York to teach at Union Theological Seminary. As his career continued at Harvard and the University of Chicago, Tillich became known as a leading existentialist theologian.

4 Linus Pauling (1901–1994).

Pauling is widely regarded as the foremost chemist of the 20th century. In 1954, he received the Nobel Prize in chemistry for his work describing chemical bonds. In addition, he received the Nobel Peace Prize in 1962 for his campaign against above-ground nuclear testing. This makes Pauling one of only two people in history (with Marie Curie) to receive two solo Nobel Prizes in two different fields.

5 Dag Hammarskjöld (1905–1961).

A Swedish economist and diplomat who became the second Secretary-General of the United Nations in April 1953. He served in that post until his death in September 1961. He was killed in a plane crash while flying to negotiate a cease-fire in the Congo and received the Nobel Peace Prize posthumously in 1961. His journals were published posthumously in a book titled *Markings,* and reflect his deep spirituality. He enjoyed being really tall.

6 Dietrich Bonhoeffer (1906–1945).

A German pastor who started an underground seminary during the Nazi period. His book *Life Together* describes this experience. Bonhoeffer participated in the plot to assassinate Hitler, was arrested, and eventually executed days before the end of the war. His *Letters and Papers from Prison* are widely influential. Known for his courage in troubled times, his receding hairline never prevented him from speaking in public.

Dietrich Bonhoeffer is perhaps the most famous Lutheran other than Martin Luther himself. Bonhoeffer worked tirelessly against the evil of his time, defining much of modern-day Lutheran ethics in the process. He never let his receding hairline trouble him.

7 Werner von Braun (1912–1977).
He received his first telescope as a confirmation gift and it propelled him to a career in rocketry. Von Braun worked for Nazi Germany and developed the V2 rockets that attacked Britain. After the war, he immigrated to the United States and developed the Saturn rockets that propelled the *Apollo* astronauts to the moon.

⑧ Jaroslav Pelikan (1923–2006).
Pelikan was born in Akron, Ohio, and graduated from the University of Chicago with a seminary degree and Ph.D. at age 22. A leading scholar of the history of Christianity, Pelikan published more than 30 books, including a five-volume *The Christian Tradition*. Though Pelikan spent most of his life a Lutheran, he was received into the Orthodox Church in America in 1998.

⑨ Martin Marty (b. 1928).
Ordained in 1952, Marty served congregations in suburban Chicago before joining the faculty of the University of Chicago in 1963. He became a leading scholar and author of more than 50 books, primarily on the history of religion in North America.

⑩ April Ulring Larson (b. 1950).
Larson was ordained as a Lutheran pastor in 1978. She was elected to serve as bishop of the La Crosse (Wisconsin) Area Synod of the Evangelical Lutheran Church in America in 1992, making her the first female Lutheran bishop in North America. Larson was re-elected to six-year terms as bishop of the La Crosse Area Synod in 1996 and 2002.

Be Aware

- Please notice the title of this entry does not read the "Ten *Most* Important Lutherans since the Reformation."

FIVE GREAT LUTHERAN COMPOSERS AND WHAT THEY WROTE

As any musician will tell you, musical "greatness" is a highly subjective designation. Over the course of Lutheran history, the church has been blessed with many talented composers.

Johann Sebastian Bach is one of the greatest composers in history and a famous Lutheran.

❶ J. S. Bach (1685–1750).
One of the greatest composers of all time, Johann
Sebastian Bach was a church musician in the German
Lutheran Church. He wrote hundreds of pieces for organ
and choir. His *Mass in B minor* and the *Brandenburg
Concertos* are perhaps his most famous works. His sons
Karl Philipp Emanuel Bach and Wilhelm Friedemann
Bach were also famous Lutheran composers.

❷ George Frederich Handel (1685–1759).
A German composer in the Baroque period who wrote
50 operas, 23 oratorios, and a lot of church music.
His most famous work is *Messiah*, which includes the
ubiquitous "Hallelujah Chorus." He also wrote *Water
Music* and *Music for the Royal Fireworks*.

❸ Johann Pachelbel (1653–1706).
Yet another German church musician and composer,
Pachelbel is credited with elevating the importance of
the organ in churches. His *Canon in D* is his most
famous work and is perhaps the most over-used piece
for wedding preludes in history.

❹ Felix Mendelssohn Bartholdy (1809–1847).
Arguably the most popular composer of the Romantic
period, Bartholdy wrote symphonies, concertos,
oratorios, piano, and chamber music. Though not
a church musician (and born into a Jewish family),
Bartholdy was drawn to Lutheranism through his study
of J. S. Bach, making him the most influential musical
convert in the church.

⑤ Martin Luther (1483–1546).
Because of his enormous influence on Christian history and theology, many people don't realize that Luther was a skilled composer and arranger of music. In 1526, his *German Mass* was instrumental (pun intended) in making changes to the liturgy. He also wrote at least 36 hymns, including "A Mighty Fortress Is Our God."

Be Aware

- Contemporary musicians with Lutheran roots include Lyle Lovett, Kris Kristofferson, John Mellencamp, and, unfortunately, David Hasselhoff.

FIVE FAMOUS LUTHERAN ARTISTS AND WHAT THEY MADE

The gospel message of freedom that Luther's Reformation recovered is known for affecting and motivating musicians and theologians to create great works, but it also spurred great minds in the arts as well. Here are just five of them.

❶ Albrecht Dürer (1471–1528).
A secret Lutheran before there was an official Lutheran church, Dürer worked for a Catholic bishop. His identification with Luther was conveyed secretly in three engravings: *Knight*, *Death,* and *Devil*.

❷ Lucas Cranach the Younger (1515–1586).
A prolific and masterful painter and printer, Cranach the Younger gave us the familiar image of Luther with his academic robe and hat and many other snapshots of the theologian's life, home, and career. Ironically, people called him Cranach the Younger even when he was old.

❸ Bertel Thorvaldsen (1770–1844).
An outstanding representative of the Neoclassical period in sculpture, Thorvaldsen worked large in size and subject. His marble statues of mythic themes, such as the famous *Lion Monument* in Lucerne, Switzerland, stand around Europe and North America, a testimony to the powerful stories of human history.

❹ Eero Saarinen (1910–1961).
This Finnish-American Lutheran set out to become a sculptor and instead became one of the most influential architects of the last century. His most recognizable design is the Gateway Arch in St. Louis, Missouri.

❺ Charles M. Schulz (1922–2000).
A Lutheran in his formative years, this artist and writer presented a very Lutheran message in his *Peanuts* comic strip. He gave us a mildly cynical view of human nature, constantly redeemed by grace stumbled upon, not found. His most famous character, Charlie Brown, coined the phrase, "AUGH!"

Eero Saarinen, a Finnish-American Lutheran and architect, designed the Gateway Arch in St. Louis, Missouri.

TOP FIVE CONTRIBUTIONS BY WOMEN OF THE CHURCH

The role of women in the church has been underdocumented and often unrecognized throughout much of the church's history. Yet women have toiled to continue Christ's mission since the beginning. Women have contributed to the church steadily and devotedly throughout the ages, summarized through these five key categories.

❶ Passing on the faith.
It was a young woman who God chose to deliver and care for the infant Messiah. Since then, women have been the driving force behind passing on the faith to countless generations of children. To this day, when only one parent is willing to take responsibility for the faith life of the family, statistically the duty falls to women, young and old.

❷ Performing ministry without acclaim.
Women have visited people who are sick and tended to those who are dying. They have provided music and song and all things that undergird worship. Without benefit of ordination, women such as 19th-century Norwegian deaconess Elizabeth Fedde established ministry sites in North America and served God where there was need.

❸ Pressing for equality: suffrage and ordination.
Women have been behind the struggle for women's ordination as well as the right to be equally represented in congregational matters. Although many Lutheran church bodies have been ordaining women for a generation and have elected female bishops, most women clergy can attest that the struggle against systemic sexism cannot yet cease.

*Women have been behind the struggle for women's
ordination as well as the right to be equally represented in
congregational matters.*

❹ Educating the church.
It is women who dominate Sunday school teacher rosters and tend to the church's faith formation systems. Although it took many years for a woman to achieve the role of leading a Lutheran seminary, it is an appropriate responsibility for the gender that has historically fueled religious education both within and without congregations.

❺ Extending Christian compassion and hospitality.
Through millions of quilts and thousands of casseroles, women have answered Christ's call to care for those in need. Whether toiling behind the scenes in basement kitchens or as individuals leading Lutheran World Relief, the World Hunger and Disaster Appeal, or the church's publishing ministry, women have done the lion's share of the church's hands-on work in the world.

SEVEN IMPORTANT LUTHERAN MISSIONARIES AND WHERE THEY WENT

A mission is a special task given to an individual or group, and a missionary is a person who performs that task. While all Christians bear the task of sharing God's love in word and deed, there have been some whose mission work has shined as a beacon for us all.

❶ Henry Melchior Muhlenberg (1711–1787).
Muhlenberg arrived from Germany in 1742 declaring Lutherans in colonial America *ecclesia plantanda*—a church yet to be planted. Miles and languages separated Lutheran settlers. Muhlenberg, the patriarch of North American Lutheranism, established "a regular ministry" by founding the Pennsylvania Ministerium, the first synod in America.

❷ William Alfred Passavant (1821–1894).
Acting on Christ's compassion, this "inner missionary" established the Pittsburg Infirmary, the first Protestant hospital in the United States, as well as many more hospitals, orphanages, and benevolent institutions. Passavant was also a leading Lutheran voice against slavery.

❸ John Christian Frederick Heyer (1793–1873).
Heyer was the first foreign missionary sent by American Lutherans. He served in India for 15 years before retiring. When the faltering mission was nearly discontinued, the 77-year-old Heyer proclaimed to the Pennsylvania Ministerium, "I am ready to go." He restored the India mission.

❹ Anna Kugler, M.D. (1856–1930).
Not only did Dr. Kugler blaze a trail for women in the medical field, she led the way for all Lutheran missionaries by serving in India. Her work there set new standards for medical missions.

❺ Maud Powlas (1889–1980).
Powlas served in Japan from 1918 until 1960, leaving only during the war years (1941–1945). She developed Jiai-en, the Lutheran Colony of Mercy, which grew into 21 ministry institutions throughout Japan.

❻ Esther Bacon (1916–1972).
Bacon delivered 20,000 babies as a midwife in Zorzor, Liberia, from 1941-1972. Under her care, the infant mortality rate there fell from 75 percent to 20 percent. She died after contracting Lassa Fever from a patient for whom she was caring.

❼ Adam Keffer (b. 1789).
In 1849, at the age of 60, Keffer walked more than 250 miles to Saegerstown, Pennsylvania, to plead for a permanent pastor to be sent to the Canadian wilderness. His great feat didn't have the desired effect so he repeated it a year later.

A BRIEF HISTORY OF THE LUTHERAN CHORAL TRADITION

Martin Luther wrote, "Next to the Word of God, music deserves the highest praise." Thus the Lutheran choral tradition began with the reformer himself—as an accomplished amateur musician and advocate of song that praises God and bears the Word. In the last five centuries, this tradition has acquired a wealth of compositions and boasts some of the greatest names in music history.

- **The 16th Century: The Beginning.**
  In addition to many familiar hymn tunes, Martin Luther composed at least one piece for *a capella* choir: *Non moriar sed vivam* ("I shall not die, but live"). Johann Walter wrote choral settings for familiar tunes and texts, such as *In dulci jubilo* and "Joseph Dearest, Joseph Mine."

- **The 17th Century: Four Sch's in the Scheventeenth Schentury.**
  Heinrich Schütz, Samuel Scheidt, and Johann Schein composed settings for one to four choirs, both *a capella* and with instruments. They introduced operatic compositional techniques to emphasize the drama in biblical texts and to intensify the German language. Michael Schultheiss, better known as Praetorius, set the familiar tunes for "On Jordan's Bank" and "Lo, How a Rose E'er Blooming."

- **The 18th Century: The Fifth Evangelist.**
  J. S. Bach's choral compositions include the range of performance options from an octet *a capella* to many voices with orchestra. He wrote mostly for the Sunday morning liturgy. He composed a different *cantata* each Sunday for nearly four church-year cycles. Bach's devotion to the

proclamation of God's word earned him the nickname of "the fifth Evangelist." He inscribed many compositions with the words *Soli Deo Gloria*, to God alone be the glory.

- **The 19th Century: A Resurrection.**
  The Age of Enlightenment caused work for professional church musicians to decline, and Lutherans rediscovered their past—the songs and faith of their tradition. With original compositions by Felix Mendelssohn Bartholdy and Johannes Brahms, amateur choirs sustained the choral tradition outside of churches. In the concert hall, Mendelssohn revived the influence of Bach, conducting a performance of Bach's *St. Matthew Passion*. Mendelssohn's revival bequeathed to generations the lasting impact of hearing and studying the maestro's works. Scandinavians went back to their roots at this time, rediscovering the spiritual tradition of their folksongs.

- **The 20th Century: The Tradition in America.**
  F. Melius Christiansen immigrated to the United States from Norway and founded the St. Olaf Choir. His influence on collegiate choirs began with his ideal choral sound—unified ensemble, perfect intonation, blend, diction, and phrasing. Most American Lutheran choirs have gone on to develop their own unique sound but will acknowledge the broad influence of Christiansen's school of singing. With this idea of tonal perfection, Christiansen raised American Lutheran choral singing to the status of concert performance. This level of musicianship and artistry leads collegiate choirs to tour the United States and the world, bringing to a variety of audiences compositions by Hugo Distler, Ernst Pepping, Carl Schalk, and Christiansen himself.

Be Aware

- Ultimately, the commitment to excellence in the art of choral singing best characterizes the Lutheran choral tradition.
- The term *a cappella* is Italian for "singing without instrumental accompaniment."
- The word *cantata* is Italian for "composition for voices and instruments, usually including a combination of solos and/or duets and choruses."
- Musicians like to use Italian. It makes them sound cosmopolitan.

Lutherans like to sing. They've been doing it for some time.

HOW TO IDENTIFY A TRADITIONAL WORSHIP DEVOTEE

Traditional worship devotees, given their uniformity in appearance and temperament, can be easy to spot. While skittish and easily spooked, calm movements, a firm handshake, and a disappointed reference to "rock 'n roll" should allow you to approach with ease.

❶ Confine your search to their native habitat: the early service.
Traditional worship devotees among Lutherans typically attend the first worship service on Sunday morning. Sociologists have identified a direct correlation between "morning people" and traditional worship devotees.

❷ Look for extreme consistency in liturgical style.
Traditionalists tend to achieve variety in worship styles by switching between Setting I and Setting II in *Lutheran Book of Worship*, if they have adopted it already. This crazy switching back and forth between settings is considered risky, "out there" behavior among many traditionalists. Familiarize yourself with the old red book (*Service Book & Hymnal*) just in case.

❸ Camouflage yourself in plain, semi-formal earth tones.
You can move more easily among traditionalists if you avoid casual or colorful clothing. Nordic sweaters and colors that match the liturgical season are the only exceptions.

Listen for the sound of ancient musical instruments. A forced-air-controlled device known as a "pipe organ" may be present where traditional worship devotees congregate. Some speculate they are attracted by the vibrations that result from notes struck at the lower end of the scale.

Traditional worship devotees tend to regard the use of multiple worship settings within a single congregation to be risky, "out-there" behavior and often favor the old "red book" (Service Book & Hymnal).

⑤ Use slow, controlled physical movements. Do not deviate from the printed material you're given. Traditionalists maintain a still, "coiled" physical posture during worship unless otherwise directed. Raising one's hands in praise is strictly forbidden unless it's part of the plan as printed in the bulletin.

⑥ Locate the alpha worshiper. Traditionalists tend only to follow a pastor when he or she is wearing a clerical collar and become disoriented at the sight of a bare-necked clergyperson. Their sense of security increases, however, at the sight of a stole, an alb, and a pectoral cross and continues to increase geometrically the more ceremonial garb is present. Paraments and candles further boost the comfort level.

⑦ Note a dearth of modern technology. Projection screens, projectors, electric instruments or amplification, soundboards, and microphones may be conspicuously absent from the traditionalists' environment, as the electronic whirring and buzzing becomes onerous to their sensitive ears. Look instead for acoustical, manual, water-and-foot pump-driven technology.

Be Aware

- "Traditional" means carried-forward. Martin Luther carried forward many of the treasures of the church's worship life—music, painting and sculpture, liturgy— unlike other reformers who rejected these elements. Healthy worship carries forward healthy tradition but doesn't worship it.

HOW TO IDENTIFY A CONTEMPORARY WORSHIP DEVOTEE

At first glance contemporary devotees may look similar to traditional worship devotees. The differences are often subtle, so careful observation is necessary. Generally, liturgical looseness, randomness, and disaffection for "the rules" mark this Lutheran.

❶ Avoid using age as a measure.
Many observers make the mistake of believing contemporary worship devotees are always young in age. As with the traditionalists, age is not a factor. Many older adults gravitate to the later worship times, frenetic music style, casual dress, and unstructured spirituality of contemporary worship.

❷ Prepare for spontaneous clapping, hand raising, and possible flailing.
The loud, rhythmic pounding of contemporary praise music often triggers spontaneous clapping, in rhythm, without prompting. Certain members of the assembly may hoot. The end of a song may be marked by scattered to thunderous applause. During prayer, hands may shoot skyward. Remain calm.

❸ Look for large images and glaring projection screens.
Some people believe it is because they tire easily with the printed word that contemporary worship devotees typically project images, moving pictures, and sometimes even text (short words, large print) on oversized screens.

Contemporary worship devotees often display a disaffection for "the rules" of worship and may spontaneously raise their hands, clap, and possibly flail.

❹ Identify the source of the rhythmic sounds. Consider protective ear wear.

A "band," composed of contemporary devotees wielding electrically fueled instruments such as guitars, drums, and keyboards may be present. It is speculated that this volume of noise is employed as a defense mechanism against traditionalists, who have sensitive hearing.

⑤ Look for chameleon-like adaptability.
Contemporary devotees exhibit a high tolerance for change, and may even delight in it. Modern translations, alternate versions of liturgical components, variety in sermon styles, and even variations on seating configurations are all accepted.

⑥ Listen for languages other than German, Norwegian, and Swedish.
Contemporary Lutheran worship songs can arise from sources all over the globe. Devotees often strive to sing them in the original languages to achieve a treasured "authenticity." Among the tongues you may hear are Spanish, Tanzanian, and Japanese.

⑦ Follow their lead regarding physical movement.
Ultimately, success among the contemporaneans depends upon your own adaptability. Besides swaying to the music, there may be a prayer path to walk, ritual actions like lighting candles, or travel between worship stations. Consider stretching exercises beforehand.

Be Aware

- "Contemporary" means up-to-date. Martin Luther transposed the timeless form and beauty of the mass into the language of the worshiping community. The result was a liturgy that was contemporary, yet traditional. Contemporary worship invites us to keep bringing the liturgy into the language of the people today.

HOW TO USHER

Ushers are the front line of a welcoming ministry. Because they prefer to practice their craft largely out of the spotlight, however, ushers are widely misunderstood. The pastor preaches and the organist plays, but without the usher nothing begins or ends and chaos ensues. Consider these guidelines before taking up the mantle.

❶ Practice scrupulous punctuality.
A late usher is a contradiction in terms. When an usher arrives disheveled and confused, it frightens worshipers and risks anarchy. People require dependable ushers to navigate the sometimes high-tension environment of corporate worship. The usher distributes bulletins and helps to seat people who arrive late.

❷ Exercise regularly; keep physically fit.
Response times in worship settings make all the difference. A slow usher allows critical situations to grow, while an agile one nips them in the bud.

❸ Employ a "soft touch" with people. Avoid becoming overzealous.
Many ushers, like mall security, give in to the trappings of the office and take a "commando" approach to their job. They see worshipers as an enemy to be contained, which leads to bad decisions in a crisis and a dissolution of trust. A better approach is to guide worshipers with kindness.

4 Use eye contact, eyebrow raises, and hand gestures judiciously.

The usher's glance indicates a time for change. While waiting for communion, a simple glance indicates the time to receive the body and blood of Christ. A premature glance can cause great confusion. Make sure eye contact is intentional and directive without being dictatorial.

Avoid becoming an overzealous or dictatorial usher.
A "soft touch" with people is more effective and nicer.

⑤ Keep calm at all times. Avoid allowing circumstances to overpower your imperturbability.

Many things go wrong in worship as a matter of course. Remain calm in the storm. It is your job to make sure the service runs smoothly and that bumps are smoothed over.

⑥ Know your duty.

The responsibilities of ushering differ from congregation to congregation. Depending on the church, you may find yourself lighting candles, bringing in Holy Communion, or passing the offering plates. Whatever the task, confidently assume appropriate authority and be ready to make godly decisions.

Be Aware

- Consider holding usher team drills at the same time the greeters hold theirs and exploit the overlap in responsibilities.
- Coordinating with clergy, lay ministers, and communion assistants to establish a rigorous system of hand gestures can facilitate cooperative leadership.

HOW TO ACOLYTE

The word *acolyte* literally means "one who follows." In the case of Lutheran worship, acolytes not only "follow" those who lead the worship service but also actually "bear the light of Christ" into the worship assembly and spread it from one candle to another. Some Lutheran congregations expect acolytes to perform many other duties as well, but experts agree that none is quite as important as stewarding the flame that denotes the Holy Spirit's presence in the assembly.

 Arrive early.
Get to the sacristy or staging area at least five minutes before start time and review the bulletin or order of service. Check in with the pastor or worship leader so they know you're ready and ask for any special instructions. For example, should the Christ (paschal) candle be lit today?

❷ **Vest properly.**
Many congregations provide special robes for their acolytes. Find a robe that fits well, as loose robes can accidentally catch fire quite easily or cause you to trip. Different styles vary in size, but typically the hem should hang about three inches above the tops of your shoes, and the sleeves should extend only to your wrists.
Note: If your congregation does not provide acolytes' robes, dress in a fashion appropriate for that service.

3 Possess yourself of the acolyte's taper (candle lighter).
Make sure you have sufficient wick, or taper, to complete your task without it burning out. If the taper is shorter than three inches, install a new one. Clean any clumpy or carbonized candle wax from the bell (the thing you use to extinguish candles, opposite the taper tip) with a non-metallic implement such as a plastic spoon.

4 Begin your tasks prayerfully.
Consider a classic Acolyte's Prayer as you move around the altar to light the candles. For example, "Jesus, you are the Light of the World. Amen."

5 Maintain a reverent frame of mind throughout the service. Participate.
Show "awesome respect" for the worship space and your important role before all the people. Avoid carrying the candle lighter like a knapsack or hockey stick. Carry it across your body in front of you with both hands, taper end angled higher than the handle end. Sit up straight and participate in the whole service.

6 Assist with communion preparation and distribution, when called upon to do so.
Congregational expectations for acolytes vary with respect to the Lord's Supper. Offering the common cup, gathering empty wine cups, and managing the flow of communicants are among the possible duties.

Receive the offering from the ushers, if it is your congregation's tradition.

Many congregations expect acolytes to receive the offering plates. Keep in mind that you are performing a holy task and, more than mere money, you hold in your hands portions of people's lives that they are giving back to God.

8 Extinguish the candles at the conclusion of the worship service.

The exact moment depends on your church's tradition. Carefully "snuff" the flame of each candle you lit in the beginning, remembering the light of Christ still is bright in your heart all through the week.

Be Aware

- Wear light clothing under your robe. A hooded sweatshirt or sweater will make you feel overheated and look oversized.
- Even if you wear "street" clothes, choose your best shoes and tie the laces. Your shoes are all that shows under your robe.
- When igniting a candelabrum, light the uppermost candle first and work your way down. When the paschal candle is lit, ignite it first and extinguish it last.
- Familiarizing yourself with the names and purposes of items in the worship space can prevent embarrassing moments during the service. When the pastor asks you to put the offering on the credence table, you need to know where it is. (See "Glossary of Lutheran Worship Terms" on page 122.)

- Always anticipate the next order in the service. Avoid getting caught flat-footed. For example, walk to the altar or go meet the ushers to receive the offering plates. This prevents "wandering" around the chancel with the look of confusion.
- Hang up your robe. The acolyte at the next service will appreciate it.

When igniting a candelabrum, light the uppermost candle first and work your way down. When extinguishing a candelabrum, simply reverse the order.

HOW TO BE A GREETER

People coming to church want someplace to belong and a community into which they can fit. Your job as a greeter is to be a friendly face that notices everyone who comes to worship and to welcome them.

❶ Define your perimeter and make sure you have all zones covered.
Assess all points of entry to your church and deploy greeting units to cover each point whenever possible. Make this your watchword: "No one gets in without a smile from us!"

❷ Familiarize yourself and your squad with the layout of the building.
Knowing where the bathrooms and the nursery are will enable you to direct worshipers to those places quickly. Arm each squad member with a map of the building, if necessary.

❸ Deploy for maximal contact.
When the worship time arrives, position your team at entry points well in advance of their approach. When a worshiper arrives, keep your body in an open stance, with your center of gravity low, and make good eye contact with a friendly smile. If they attempt to breach your perimeter in a group (as, say, a family might do) redeploy yourself so that you can greet each person.

❹ Make appropriate physical contact.
Once within reach, offer an open hand ready for the shaking. Be genuine in your gestures and your speech, as you grip firmly and speak words of greeting, like, "Good morning!" or "Welcome to _____ *(name of church)*." Gently place any appropriate printed material—bulletins, announcements, and so on—in their hands.

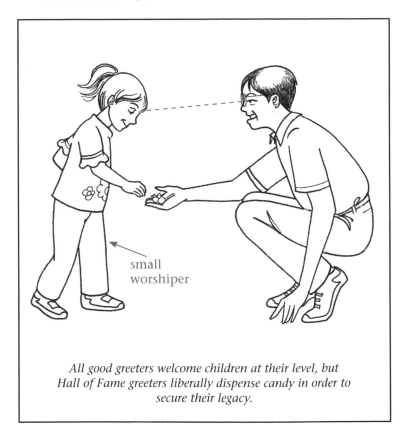

small
worshiper

All good greeters welcome children at their level, but Hall of Fame greeters liberally dispense candy in order to secure their legacy.

⑤ Greet children on their level.
When miniature worshipers are in tow, get down to their eye level and greet them in their own language. Make sure parents know where the "busy bags," or children's worship bags, are and how to find the nursery and the bathroom in a pinch.

⑥ Read the worshiper's eyes and adapt to overcome.
Some folks are not interested in being overwhelmed with smiling sunshininess first thing in the morning. Avoid lashing out with a boisterous handshake if they don't want one. Your objective is not a direct assault but simply containment and safety. A silent smile and a nod is all the greeting that most non-morning people require.

Be Aware

- The key to an effective greeting team is good training. Professional greeting teams often run drills during off-hours to prepare for every eventuality.
- Consider purchasing walkie-talkies with headsets for your squad to ensure maximum communication capability.
- Hall of Fame greeters are known to have kept a pocketful of small, individually wrapped candies and dispensed them liberally to children.
- The snack table is a security zone. Establish a perimeter around it and allow only small children to filch before the fellowship hour officially begins.

FIVE COMMON WORSHIP PRACTICES AND WHY LUTHERANS DO THEM

While some language and gestures during Lutheran worship can seem bizarre to the uninitiated, they do not indicate cultism. There is a solid, biblical reason for each one and knowing the reason can add meaning and satisfaction to your worship experience.

❶ Passing the peace.

It might seem like your weekly chance to say hello to everyone, but passing the peace is more than hand shaking and small talk. "Peace be with you" was the greeting of the risen Christ to his disciples (see John 20:19) and sharing the peace extends Jesus' blessing. The practice grew out of the "kiss of peace" (see Romans 16:16), an ancient ritual symbolizing one's close relationship to another person.

❷ Taking an offering.

Lutherans collect an offering as a tangible response to God's blessings to us. God's people for centuries have been challenged to return a tenth of their possessions (a "tithe") to the service of the Lord. An offering goes far beyond money and includes our time, energy, talents, and the use of our material possessions. We are called to offer *everything* that we have to God. But the money's pretty important.

❸ Saying, "And also with you."

The congregation generally provides this response after the worship leader gives a blessing (such as "The Lord be with you") before a prayer. To respond, "And also with you," returns the blessing to the leader, giving the message, "We're in this together."

A key way Lutherans participate actively in the worship service is by singing songs and hymns. This is an old tradition, and it still works.

❹ Singing hymns.

For much of history, worshipers participated by simply watching leaders preach, pray, sing, and celebrate Holy Communion. Martin Luther sought to broaden participation through an important component: the singing of hymns. Hymns often express the themes explored elsewhere in worship, such as in the Bible readings, sermon, or Holy Communion, while inviting the whole congregation to participate.

❺ Receiving the benediction.

A benediction is a blessing (*bene* = good, *dictio* = to say). It marks the close of the worship service and our return into the world, a reminder of God's grace and presence as we go. While there are variations, a common benediction is, "Almighty God, Father, Son, and Holy Spirit, bless you now and forever." Also common is the Aaronic Benediction, which begins: "The Lord bless you and keep you"—the blessing that Aaron gave to his fellow Israelites (see Numbers 6:22-27).

HOW TO READ SCRIPTURE ALOUD DURING WORSHIP

The Bible has been read aloud in thousands of different settings for hundreds of years. So whether you're reading the Bible aloud for the first time or for the hundredth time, these helpful hints will guide your reading and make it the best it can be.

Preparation

❶ Sit down with a Bible.
It's wise to get familiar with the reading ahead of time.

❷ Unleash your curiosity as you read.
Ask questions like: Who is speaking? Is this a story or a teaching? What is the context? Who is the audience? Where is that place? Who is that person? How do you pronounce that?

❸ Find the answers.
Use a Bible dictionary. Ask your pastor. Look up commentary about the text online. Read the stuff that comes right before the text and right after it. That might help. The point is to understand as well as you can what you are reading.

❹ Read the passage or chapter out loud to yourself.
Mark up the page so you can remember where to pause and what to emphasize.

❺ Read it out loud again.
Does it make sense now?

6 Experiment with vocal expression.

If you were telling this story instead of reading it, what would you sound like? Imagine you are reading to very young kids. Pause. Change the tone of your voice. Change the pitch.

7 Make sure the print is readable.

If the print is too small or the lines of type are too long, retype it so you can read it easily. Then remember to take the new copy with you.

Reading the Bible in public forums, like Sunday worship, requires poise and focus. But it can be a very rewarding experience.

Public Reading

❶ Arrive at the space ahead of time.
Stand where you will read. Figure out where the book or paper should be so you can see it well. If you can, try out the microphone so you know where to point your face in order to have the microphone pick up your voice.

❷ Be on the lookout for danger.
Undetected steps, podiums, electrical cords, and microphones can cause painful and embarrassing situations while standing before a large group.

❸ Mark the page.
A bookmark and/or highlighter pen will prevent you from losing your place in front of your listeners.

❹ Say a silent prayer before you begin.
Ask God to be with you as you deliver the reading, and to speak through you.

❺ Read more slowly than you imagine you should.
If you are nervous it will feel like you are crawling along, but it will probably be about right.

❻ Speak loudly and clearly enough so your voice carries.
You might have to slow down even more if the space is really big.

❼ Continue to breathe.
Public speaking is one of the average person's greatest fears, and it may result in the failure to take in enough oxygen. Gently inhale and exhale while you talk.

❽ Look up only if you feel comfortable.
It's much better to keep your eyes on the page than to lose your place.

⑨ Remember to pause.
Pause for just a moment once you get in place before you start reading. Pause for just a moment after you finish and before you leave. The pauses are kind of like bookends.

Private Reading

❶ Connect with your listener.
Before beginning to read, exchange a warm greeting, learn one another's names, and share a bit of personal information.

❷ Relax.
Your listener will appreciate your reading if done in a calm, gentle manner. If you encounter difficult words for names or places, try your best to pronounce them. Your listener will understand.

❸ Be sure the person to whom you are reading can see your face and hear your voice.

❹ Kick up the expression a bit, especially if you are reading to kids.
They won't listen if you are boring or clueless. Instead, their minds will wander, and they may even wander away —literally. The Bible can be funny and mysterious and suspenseful and sad. If your reading carries an emotion, read it like it does.

HOW TO CHANT

The tradition of chanting—intoning certain portions of the worship liturgy within a limited range of notes—dates back many centuries. Prior to the invention of PA systems, chanting originally was used because intonations carry further in large churches or cathedrals than spoken words do. Lutheran chanting ranges in quality from abysmal to superlative. While all chanting is pleasing to the Lord, it's not always pleasing to human ears.

❶ Prepare and practice well in advance.
Look over the liturgical sections, giving careful consideration to the meaning of the words and the structure of the sentences. In a chant, conveying the text clearly is most important.

❷ Commit the musical underlayment of your piece to memory.
Play (or have played for you) the musical notes on a piano or other instrument. Do this repeatedly without the words until the tune can be sung without accompaniment.

❸ Practice the chant until it becomes second nature.
Note that the rhythm is determined by the text itself. Give emphasis and duration to the most important words in the text, regardless of note value.

❹ Focus on your breathing.
Good breath support is important. Use enough air to sing a resonant tone, but each line should be sung without stopping to take a breath.

Spoken words can be difficult to hear.

Chanting ensures that everyone can hear.

The tradition of chanting—intoning certain portions of the worship liturgy within a limited range of notes—dates back many centuries and was done so people could hear the words.

⑤ Sing the vowels of the words.
Don't hold pitch on an *r* or *n*, but be sure to enunciate the consonants so that the words can be readily understood.

⑥ Keep an upright but relaxed posture.
Avoid slouching. Likewise, avoid standing ramrod straight, as this will probably cause you to pass out.

Be Aware

- Chant is considered "plainsong," which means that vibrato and other musical expressions are minimized. Sing only a plain, pure constant note to carry the text.
- A "chanter" and a "cantor" are basically the same thing, except a cantor may be a member of the choir and sing a solo from time to time. Fancy people say "cantor," but the terms "soloist" or "leader" may also be used.
- The late theologian Joseph Sittler observed that many chanters appear to change the liturgical sound to, "Let us *bray* to the Lord." Training and practice can help avoid this judgment.

HOW TO SET THE COMMUNION TABLE

Any dinner party should have its table set properly. One can expect to find forks resting to the left of the dinner plate, with the smaller salad fork on the outside and the fork for the main course on the inside. Just as there are guidelines for setting a dinner table, so there are guidelines for setting the communion table.

❶ Say a prayer of preparation.
Professional altar guild members claim this step is essential and adds a valuable, intangible element to their work. Many sacristies post prayers of preparation inside a cupboard door or just to the left or right of the doorway.

❷ Examine your variables and adapt.
Is the presiding minister right-handed or left-handed? Is the altar free standing? Is this the traditional or contemporary service? What season of the church year is it? Are there special instructions for this worship service? Is there an offering procession? Attention to these details can help avoid a mishap. Stay sharp.

❸ "Vest" or dress the chalice, if your congregation keeps this particular tradition.*
a) A purificator folded in thirds lengthwise is placed over the mouth of the empty chalice so that the right and left sides hang evenly over the edges of the chalice.
b) The paten is placed on top of the purificator.

* This tradition probably arose from the practical need to keep the bread and wine protected from dust and other contaminates until ready for use.

c) The paten is covered with the pall.
d) The chalice veil in the proper color of the day is placed over the pall and arranged so that a trapezoid is seen when viewed from the front.
e) The corporal and additional purificators are placed in the burse, which matches the veil. The burse is laid on top of the vested chalice.

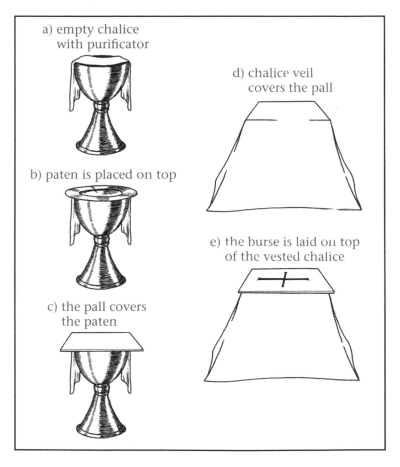

a) empty chalice with purificator

b) paten is placed on top

c) the pall covers the paten

d) chalice veil covers the pall

e) the burse is laid on top of the vested chalice

❹ Set the communion table at the offering.

- Spread the corporal in the center of the altar. The corporal is the white linen cloth, similar to a tablecloth, on which the bread and wine are placed.
- Place the paten (the plate) with bread slightly to the right on the corporal.
- Set the chalice (the cup) of wine slightly to the left on the corporal.
- Provide a few small cloths, known as purificators. Purificators function as napkins to catch any possible drips of wine.

The following arrangement is appropriate when a whole loaf of bread is used:

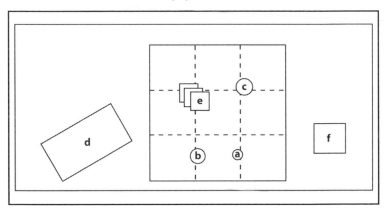

a) paten
b) chalice
c) flagon or cruet
d) missal stand
e) purificators
f) burse

If hosts are used, the following arrangement may be employed:

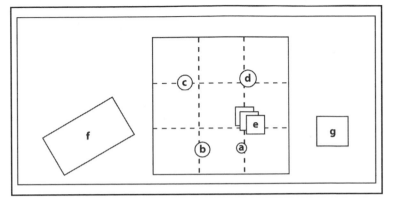

a) paten
b) chalice
c) ciborium or host box
d) flagon or cruet
e) purificators
f) missal stand
g) burse

Be Aware

- While a well-set communion table can add meaning to the rite of Holy Communion, Lutherans believe only the bread, wine, and God's word are *necessary* for the sacrament to do its work.
- Communion ware can be constructed of nearly any material. Stone, pottery, wood, brass, silver, glass, and even gold are not uncommon. The gold is usually just gold plating, though.
- When setting the table, keep in mind that variations are acceptable. A well-trained altar guild member can make any altar look snappy and function well. Remain adaptable and flexible to your circumstances.

HOW TO ASSIST DURING COMMUNION DISTRIBUTION

Assisting the pastor(s) in distributing communion to the congregation during worship is an honor and a privilege, so don't blow it by acting goofy. But also keep in mind that God is lavishly pouring out his Son in the bread and wine to sinners who need their Savior, which is a joyous, poignant moment. Don't blow it by being a stuffed shirt either.

❶ Keep in mind that you are part of something holy and joyous. Act accordingly.
Especially when serving communion to kneeling individuals, interesting jewelry, ties, or fancy clothes can serve as a distraction. Keep your mind on your game plan to avoid spills. On the other hand, avoid frowning. Communion is happy.

❷ Enter into your duty calm, confident, and relaxed. Remain flexible.
Learn your role, route, and the method of distribution well prior to worship. Wear comfortable shoes. Maintain visual contact with ushers and clergy, and be ready to respond to hand signals. Allow your physical presence to communicate assurance to communicants.

❸ Look individuals in the eye and speak clearly.
If serving the bread, say in a firm, steady voice, "The body of Christ, given for you." If serving wine or grape juice say, "The blood of Christ, shed for you." Avoid chitchat. **Note:** Some congregations hold the tradition of adding the individual's name at this point whenever possible. Do not use someone's name unless you're absolutely sure what it is.

Even during communion distribution, in the traditional manner it is important to look individuals in the eye and speak the words, "Given and shed for you," clearly.

❹ Mobilize to deliver the sacrament to the less ambulatory.
Take the elements to individuals who are not physically able to come to you, unless your church uses a different method.

⑤ Prepare ahead of time for shortages and mishaps.
When mishaps occur, move nimbly and discreetly.
Calmly locate back-up elements before running short.
Promptly and quietly pick up elements that drop to
the ground; do not mix them back in. Remove foreign
objects from the wine with a linen napkin or small,
slotted spoon, not your finger.

⑥ Practice good personal hygiene.
Keep in mind that you are serving a meal. Wash your
hands immediately before assisting with communion. In
a pinch, a discreet pump of antibacterial "germ gel" will
suffice. Many altar guilds strategically place small bottles
of hand sanitizer around the chancel area.

Be Aware

- Communion is a sacrament of grace; all are welcome
  regardless of age or understanding. Local customs and
  family traditions, however, vary. To determine if children
  are communing, look for hand and eye cues. In a pinch,
  ask a parent.
- Noncommuning children often receive a blessing and
  the sign of the cross.

HOW TO DELIVER COMMUNION TO A HOMEBOUND PERSON

Distributing communion to homebound persons is not simply meals-on-wheels for the sacrament, but a time to show individuals that they are remembered and cared for by the congregation and can be a vital lifeline to once-active members. Always check with the pastor about your church's customs.

❶ Prepare the elements for a road trip.
Church supply stores stock communion kits, but homemade versions can suffice. Bring cups and wine or grape juice, along with bread or wafers. Include extras to offer to others present. Elements from corporate worship are often used. Check with your pastor before launching out alone.

❷ Assemble recent congregational communications for delivery.
Before leaving the church facility, gather appropriate items, such as recent bulletins and large-print devotionals, if fitting. People who are homebound rely on these materials to stay up-to-date and informed regarding their church home.

❸ Call ahead.
There's nothing worse than visiting a homebound person and finding that the individual is not home. A quick phone call to confirm your visit can avoid embarrassing calendar conflicts. Unexpected visits can also expose bad hair, lack of makeup, and unshavenness.

Dress in layers.

Often, persons with health concerns and older adults may prefer a warmer thermostat setting. You may find the house a sauna, or you may find it an icebox. Be prepared.

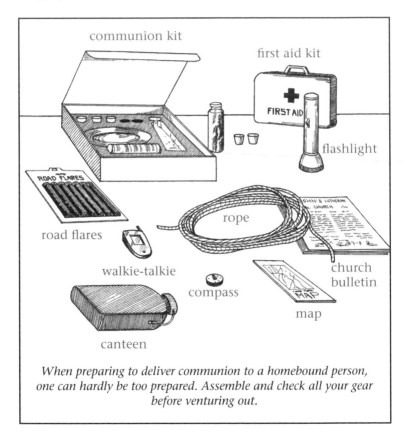

communion kit

first aid kit

FIRST AID

flashlight

ROAD FLARES

rope

road flares

JOHN'S LUTHERAN
CHURCH

church bulletin

walkie-talkie

compass

MAP

map

canteen

When preparing to deliver communion to a homebound person, one can hardly be too prepared. Assemble and check all your gear before venturing out.

❺ Prepare yourself mentally for an unfamiliar environment.
Entering another's home can prove taxing. Do not judge. Surprises may include unique odors, clutter, and occasionally open-robed hosts. Fresh air may be nominal, especially in a smoker's residence. A lingering welcome in an open doorway circulates fresh air.

❻ Pray and read Scripture aloud with the person.
After a time of conversation and preparation of the elements, offer prayer. Include the Lord's Prayer. Clergy may use this time to say the words of institution.

❼ Distribute communion according to an established and familiar ritual.
Speak to your pastor or worship committee about obtaining individually printed rites of distribution. Always say, "The body of Christ, given for you," and "The blood of Christ, shed for you."

Be Aware

- Your presence and prayers are a ministry, but as Jesus could surely testify, ministry is not always appreciated. Individuals suffering from loneliness, depression, or pain may not convey gratitude. Your reward may be in heaven.

HOW TO DELIVER A TEMPLE TALK/MAKE AN ANNOUNCEMENT DURING WORSHIP

Church leaders and members are often asked to give a brief message or announcement at a worship service. Even though these presentations are usually short and informal, they should be taken seriously and approached with careful planning.

❶ Know your audience.
Be sure you have a good understanding of who will be present at the worship service, including their age range, gender, values, and concerns. If you're in doubt, talk to your pastor.

❷ Get your message clearly in mind.
Consult with the person who assigned the talk to you. Be certain of the specific purpose and the basic message that is to be conveyed. Avoid long deviations into personal anecdotes.

❸ Focus your message.
Develop a thesis statement that conveys the basic message in a way that would appeal to an individual from this audience. The thesis should be a single declarative sentence.

❹ Assemble a limited number of illustrations or examples.
Expand the thesis into no more than two or three main points. Support each point with one or two *brief* subpoints.

❺ Prepare an outline.
Rather than a word-for-word manuscript, use the time-honored short outline method. Don't take anything larger than a small index card with you. This will enable you to speak naturally and conversationally, rather than with a reader's voice, especially if you've memorized your talk.

❻ Practice the speech at least a half-dozen times.
Enlist a spouse, friends, or other church members as a sample audience that can offer frank feedback. Time the speech in rehearsal. Make every effort to keep the length at less than three minutes unless you have been asked to speak for a longer time.

When delivering a temple talk to the congregation it is sometimes advisable to outline your thoughts on index cards, which are portable and relatively unobtrusive.

IMPORTANT INSTITUTIONS EVERY

Institution	Members or supporters
The Canadian Council of Churches	20 churches and organizations, including the ELCIC
Lutheran Disaster Response	The ELCA and Lutheran Church—Missouri Synod (LCMS)
Lutheran Immigration and Refugee Service	The ELCA, LCMS, and Latvian Evangelical Lutheran Church in America
Lutheran Services in America	The ELCA, LCMS, and related social ministry organizations
The Lutheran World Federation	140 denominations (including the ELCA and ELCIC) in 78 countries, representing 66.2 million Christians
Lutheran World Relief	ELCA and LCMS
National Council of Churches USA	35 denominations (including the ELCA), representing 45 million Christians
The World Council of Churches	340 denominations (including the ELCA and ELCIC) and church fellowships in more than 100 countries and territories, representing 550 million Christians

LUTHERAN SHOULD KNOW ABOUT

Mission	Web site
Studies and addresses issues of faith and witness, justice and peace, and biotechnology.	www.ccc-cce.ca
Provides aid and long-term recovery services for those affected in domestic disasters.	www.ldr.org
Advocates for and welcomes refugees and immigrants.	www.lirs.org
Coordinates the ministries of more than 300 social service agencies in the U.S. and Caribbean.	www.lutheranservices.org
Focuses on humanitarian assistance, mission and development, theological research, international affairs and human rights, and ecumenical relations.	www.lutheranworld.org
Works with partners in 35 countries to help people grow food, improve health, strengthen communities, end conflict, build livelihoods, and recover from disasters.	www.lwr.org
Promotes mutual understanding and collaboration on programs for education, advocacy, and service.	www.ncccusa.org
Explores issues of faith and order; mission and ecumenical formation; justice, peace, and creation; international affairs, peace, and human security; and service and solidarity.	www.wcc-coe.org

THE LUTHERAN FAMILY TREE

Each of the four largest Lutheran churches in North America has arrived in today's world after a long journey that often began with boatloads of immigrant Lutherans from central and northern Europe. Each has some identifying marks that can often help you know which Lutheran family you're encountering.

No matter which Lutheran church body you visit, you can be sure that in each the primary Lutheran teaching of Christ's justification of the ungodly will be present, because each church points to the Lutheran Confessions as central to its identity.

Key (to chart on following pages):

 Has a wide range of ecumenical partners and agreements

 Engaged in ecumenical partnerships but having few official agreements

Fellowship limited to other Lutheran churches in doctrinal agreement, but engaged in joint ministry project

Fellowship limited to other Lutheran churches in doctrinal agreement. Does not engage in joint ministry activities

 Pastors are male

 Pastors are both male and female

 Bishops oversee geographical jurisdictions

 District presidents oversee geographical jurisdictions

Lay deacons engage in ministry of service

Laypeople live the gospel in their daily lives

THE LUTHERAN FAMILY TREE

Logo	Acronym	Full name	First Lutheran in this line	Ethnicity of founding members	
	ELCA	Evangelical Lutheran Church in America	1638: Immigrants in New Sweden in the Delaware Valley	German, Scandinavian, Slovak	
	ELCIC	Evangelical Lutheran Church in Canada	1619: Rasmus Jensen, first Lutheran pastor in North America	German, Scandinavian	
	LCMS	The Lutheran Church— Missouri Synod	1839: Immigrants from Saxony in Germany	German	
	WELS	Wisconsin Evangelical Lutheran Synod	1837: Pastor John Mühlhäuser, immigrant to Wisconsin	German	

Bible	Ecumenical fellowship	Ministry	Headquarters	Influential theologians
The source and norm for Christian life			Chicago, Illinois	Henry Melchior Muhlenberg, Samuel Schmucker, J. Michael Reu, Franklin Clark Fry
Inspired and authoritative standard for the church's life			Winnipeg, Manitoba	William E. Hordern, Roger Nostbakken, Otto W. Heick, Faith Rohrbough
Contains no errors. All parts contain the infallible truth.			St. Louis, Missouri	C. F. W. Walther, Franz Pieper, J.A.O. Preus
Fully inspired and inerrant			Milwaukee, Wisconsin	John Philip Koehler and the Wauwautosa theologians

A BRIEF HISTORY OF THE LUTHERAN MOVEMENT

Martin Luther didn't like the fact that his "followers" were being called Lutherans: "How is it that I—poor, stinking bag of maggots that I am—should have people call the children of Christ by my wretched name?" For better or worse, the "Lutheran" moniker stuck. Here's a brief history of the Lutheran movement and its continuing spread.

1483 Martin Luther born in Eisleben, Germany.

1505 Luther quits law school and enters the monastery.

1512 Luther begins teaching at Wittenberg University, lecturing on the Bible.

1517 Luther posts the *Ninety-five Theses on the Power and Efficacy of Indulgences*.

1518 Philipp Melanchthon joins the Wittenberg faculty.

1521 Luther's famous stand at the Diet of Worms.

1523 The first Lutheran martyrs: Two Lutheran monks burned at the stake in Brussels.

King Gustavus Vasa begins spread of Lutheran movement to Sweden and Finland.

1529 Small and Large Catechisms published.

Lutherans debate Zwinglians at Marburg; subject: Where's Jesus in the Lord's Supper?

Lutherans and other reformers labeled "Protestants" as Diet of Speier.

1530   Melanchthon drafts the Augsburg Confession (presented at the Diet of Augsburg).

Later, Melanchthon publishes a defense (*Apologia*) of the articles of the Augsburg Confession.

1537   Two more Confessional Documents, *The Smalcald Articles* (by Luther) and *On the Power and Primacy of the Pope* (by Melanchthon) are published.

Denmark becomes officially Lutheran (and with it, eventually, Norway).

1546   Luther dies in Eisleben.

1548   The controversial "Leipzig Interim" attempts a compromise with Rome in the face of the Smalcald War begun earlier that year.

1555   "The Peace of Augsburg" allows territorial rulers to establish either the Lutheran or Roman Catholic confession in their lands (this according to the principle of *cuius regio eius religio* = "whose territory, his religion").

1560   Melanchthon dies in Wittenberg.

1580   "The Formula of Concord" is published in attempt to settle inter-Lutheran disputes once and for all. Nice try. The "Formula" is included in *The Book of Concord*, which includes the Augsburg Confession and other key Lutheran documents. *The Book of Concord* helps usher in a period of "Lutheran Orthodoxy" in Germany.

1620   Rasmus Jensen, the first Lutheran pastor sent to the "New World" (from Denmark) dies near what is now Churchill, Manitoba.

1648   "The Peace of Westphalia" ends the brutal Thirty Years War between various Protestant and Roman Catholic forces.

1649   First Lutheran Church, Albany, New York, founded by Dutch settlers; it is the first officially organized Lutheran church in what would become the United States.

1675   Philip Jacob Spener's little book *Pia Desideria* ("Pious Desires") launches the Pietist movement. The subtitle of his book describes this movement well: "Heartfelt Yearnings for the God-pleasing Improvement of the True Evangelical Church."

1723   Johann Sebastian Bach becomes Director of Music in Leipzig; for Lutherans, Bach represents the epitome of combining sound biblical theology with the church's worship and choral music (see Bach's *St. Matthew's Passion*).

1817   In an early attempt at enforced ecumenism, King Frederick William III organizes Lutheran and Reformed Christians into the "Prussian Union."

1847   German immigrant and pastor C. F. W. Walther named first president of the newly formed Lutheran Church—Missouri Synod.

1933   In response to the formation of Hitler's Reich Church, pastors like Dietrich Bonhoeffer and Martin Niemöller form the underground "Confessing Church."

1947   The Lutheran World Federation (LWF) is organized in the aftermath of World War II. In 2006, the LWF membership included 140 different Lutheran church bodies, in 78 different countries, representing about 66 million Lutheran Christians.

1987   The Evangelical Lutheran Church in America is formed; the ELCA represents a merger of predecessor Lutheran churches of primarily Swedish, Norwegian, and German heritage.

The history of the Lutheran movement is rich with colorful characters and inspiring stories. C. F. W. Walther was the first president of the Missouri Synod and wore bushy sideburns and a neck beard, which were fashionable in 1847.

COMMON TYPES OF LUTHERAN CLERGY GARB

Clergy in different Lutheran traditions wear different clothing in their work. Each serves a particular function.

The alb and stole represent the Holy Spirit's presence and the yoke of Christ.

In some traditions, clergy emphasize the academic side of pastoring and interpreting the Bible, often wearing academic-style robes.

stole

academic robe with chevrons

alb

In some traditions, a clergyperson of higher authority, such as a bishop, may wear a miter. The chasuble typically is worn for celebrating Holy Communion and may be worn by pastors, too.

To signify their role among their congregants and the universal nature of Christian ministry, some clergy dress in sharp suits.

miter

chasuble

sharp suit

NAMES FOR LUTHERAN WORSHIP FURNISHINGS, MINISTERS, PARAMENTS, AND VESTMENTS

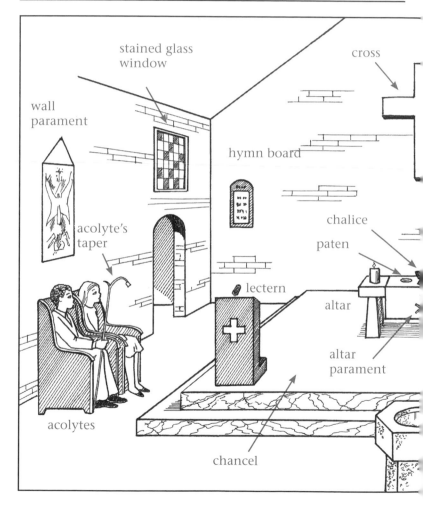

stained glass window

cross

wall parament

hymn board

acolyte's taper

chalice

paten

lectern

altar

altar parament

acolytes

chancel

paschal candle

projection screen

pulpit

assisting minister

pulpit parament

baptismal font

pastor/ presiding minister

SING TO THE LORD, O MY SOUL!

LUTHERAN DENOMINATIONS IN NORTH AMERICA

It is easy to forget how many different kinds of Lutherans there are in the world, but the church that was born for reform evidently can't stop doing so. Oftentimes, when a group of Lutherans attempts reform within their denomination some of them want it to stay the way it was, so they wind up with two denominations instead of one. Conversely, two distinct denominations sometimes decide they have too much in common to continue separately and they join together. In the end, all one can do is marvel at the grand variety of Lutherans that God has allowed there to be.

American Association of Lutheran Churches
Headquarters: Minneapolis, Minnesota
Congregations: 86
Founded: 1987

Apostolic Lutheran Church of America
Headquarters: Battle Ground, Washington
Congregations: 46

Association of Free Lutheran Congregations
Headquarters: Plymouth, Minnesota
Congregations: 250
Founded: 1962

Association of Independent Evangelical Lutheran Churches
Headquarters: Astoria, New York
Congregations: 55
Founded: 2001

Canadian Association of
Lutheran Congregations
    Headquarters: Kamloops,
    British Columbia
    Congregations: 3
    Founded: 1991

Church of the Lutheran
Brethren of America
    Headquarters: Fergus Falls,
    Minnesota
    Congregations: 120
    Founded: 1900

Church of the Lutheran
Confession
    Headquarters: Eau Claire,
    Wisconsin
    Congregations: 77
    Founded: 1960

Concordia Lutheran
Conference
    Headquarters: Seattle,
    Washington
    Congregations: 8
    Founded: 1951

Estonian Evangelical
Lutheran Church Abroad
    Headquarters: Toronto,
    Ontario
    Congregations: 63
    Founded: 1947

Evangelical Lutheran
Church in America
    Headquarters: Chicago,
    Illinois
    Congregations: 10,657
    Founded: 1988

Evangelical Lutheran
Church in Canada
    Headquarters: Winnipeg,
    Manitoba
    Congregations: 624
    Founded: 1986

Evangelical Lutheran
Conference and Ministerium
of North America
    Headquarters: Altoona,
    Pennsylvania
    Congregations: 7
    Founded: 1992

Evangelical Lutheran Synod
    Headquarters: Mankato,
    Minnesota
    Founded: 1955

Fellowship of Confessing
Lutheran Churches
    Headquarters: Bay Shore,
    New York
    Congregations: 2
    Founded: 2001

International Lutheran Fellowship, Inc.
>Headquarters: Springfield, Illinois
>Founded: 1967

Laestadian Lutheran Church
>Headquarters: Loretto, Minnesota
>Congregations: 29
>Founded: 1973

Lithuanian Evangelical Lutheran Church in Diaspora
>Headquarters: Oak Park, Illinois
>Founded: 1897

Lutheran Church—Canada
>Headquarters: Winnipeg, Manitoba
>Congregations: 328
>Founded: 1988

Lutheran Church—Missouri Synod
>Headquarters: St. Louis, Missouri
>Congregations: 6,150
>Founded: 1847

Protest'ant Conference
>Headquarters: Appleton, Wisconsin
>Congregations: 6
>Founded: 1927

Lutheran Churches of the Reformation
>Headquarters: Fort Wayne, Indiana
>Congregations: 15
>Founded: 1964

Lutheran Congregations in Mission for Christ
>Headquarters: Canton, Michigan
>Congregations: 117
>Founded: 2001

Lutheran Evangelical Protestant Church
>Headquarters: West Columbia, South Carolina
>Congregations: 44
>Founded: 2001

Lutheran Ministerium and Synod–USA
Headquarters: Indianapolis, Indiana
Congregations: 4
Founded: 1995

Lutheran Orthodox Church
Headquarters: Neffs, Pennsylvania
Congregations: 89
Founded: 2001

Wisconsin Evangelical Lutheran Synod
Headquarters: Milwaukee, Wisconsin
Congregations: 1,261
Founded: 1850

LUTHERAN COLLEGES AND UNIVERSITIES IN NORTH AMERICA

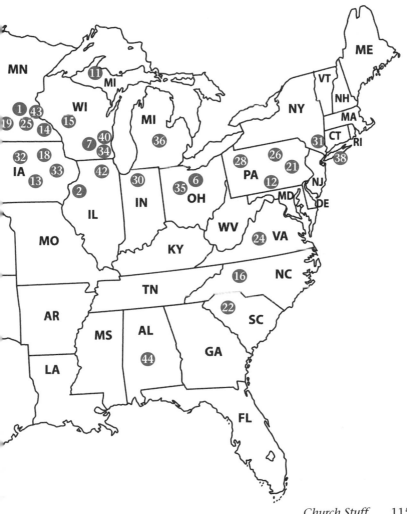

1. Augsburg College, Minneapolis, Minnesota (ELCA)

2. Augustana, Rock Island, Illinois (ELCA)

3. Augustana, Sioux Falls, South Dakota (ELCA)

4. Bethany College, Lindsborg, Kansas (ELCA)

5. California Lutheran University, Thousand Oaks, California (ELCA)

6. Capital University, Columbus, Ohio (ELCA)

7. Carthage College, Kenosha, Wisconsin (ELCA)

8. Concordia College University of Alberta, Edmonton, Alberta (LCC)

9. Concordia College, Moorhead, Minnesota (ELCA)

10. Dana College, Blair, Nebraska (ELCA)

11. Finlandia University, Hancock, Michigan (ELCA)

12. Gettysburg College, Gettysburg, Pennsylvania (ELCA)

13. Grand View College, Des Moines, Iowa (ELCA)

14. Gustavus Adolphus College, St. Peter, Minnesota (ELCA)

15. Immanuel Lutheran College, Eau Claire, Wisconsin (CLC)

16. Lenoir-Rhyne College, Hickory, North Carolina (ELCA)

17. Luther College at the University of Regina, Regina, Saskatchewan (ELCIC)

18. Luther College, Decorah, Iowa (ELCA)

19. Martin Luther College, New Ulm, Minnesota (WELS)

20. Midland Lutheran College, Fremont, Nebraska (ELCA)

21. Muhlenberg College, Allentown, Pennsylvania (ELCA)

22. Newberry College, Newberry, South Carolina (ELCA)

23. Pacific Lutheran University, Tacoma, Washington (ELCA)

24. Roanoke College, Salem, Virginia (ELCA)

25. St. Olaf College, Northfield, Minnesota (ELCA)

26. Susquehanna University, Selinsgrove, Pennsylvania (ELCA)

27. Texas Lutheran University, Seguin, Texas (ELCA)

28. Thiel College, Greenville, Pennsylvania (ELCA)

29. Trinity Lutheran College, Issaquah, Washington (independent)

30. Valparaiso University, Valparaiso, Indiana (independent)

31. Wagner College, Staten Island, New York (ELCA)

32. Waldorf College, Forest City, Iowa (ELCA)

33. Wartburg College, Waverly, Iowa (ELCA)

34. Wisconsin Lutheran College, Milwaukee, Wisconsin (WELS)

35. Wittenberg University, Springfield, Ohio (ELCA)

The Concordia University System (LCMS) includes these campuses:

36. Concordia University, Ann Arbor, Michigan

37. Concordia University at Austin, Austin, Texas

38. Concordia College—New York, Bronxville, New York

39. Concordia University Irvine, Irvine, California

40. Concordia University Wisconsin, Mequon, Wisconsin

41. Concordia University, Portland, Oregon

42. Concordia University Chicago, River Forest, Illinois

43. Concordia University, St. Paul, Minnesota

44. Concordia College, Selma, Alabama

45. Concordia University Nebraska, Seward, Nebraska

Some prominent Lutheran Colleges and Universities outside North America:

Australia Lutheran College, Adelaide, Australia

Universidade Luterana do Brasil (Ulbra), Canoas, Rio Grande do Sul, Brazil

Immanuel Lutheran College, Hong Kong, China

Tumaini University, Tanzania

Lutheran Theological Seminaries in North America:

Association of Free Lutheran Theological Seminary, Plymouth, Minnesota

Bethany Lutheran Theological Seminary, Mankato, Minnesota (WELS)

Concordia Lutheran Theological Seminary, St. Catharines, Ontario (LCC)

Concordia Seminary, St. Louis, Missouri (LCMS)

Concordia Theological Seminary, Fort Wayne, Indiana (LCMS)

Faith Evangelical Lutheran Seminary, Tacoma, Washington

Luther Seminary, St. Paul, Minnesota (ELCA)

Lutheran Brethren Seminary, Fergus Falls, Minnesota

Lutheran School of Theology at Chicago (ELCA)

Lutheran Theological Seminary at Gettysburg (ELCA)

The Lutheran Theological Seminary at Philadelphia (ELCA)

Lutheran Theological Seminary, Saskatoon, Saskatchewan (ELCIC)

Lutheran Theological Southern Seminary, Columbia, South Carolina (ELCA)

Pacific Lutheran Theological Seminary, Berkeley, California (ELCA)

Trinity Lutheran Seminary, Columbus, Ohio (ELCA)

Wartburg Theological Seminary, Dubuque, Iowa (ELCA)

Waterloo Lutheran Seminary, Waterloo, Ontario (ELCIC)

Wisconsin Lutheran Seminary, Mequon, Wisconsin (WELS)

Some prominent Lutheran Theological Seminaries outside North America:

Lutheran Theological Seminary, Novosibirsk, Russia

Norwegian School of Theology Menighetsfakultet (MF)

Paulinum Seminary, Windhoek, Namibia

Saint Sophia Ukrainian Lutheran Theological Seminary, Velyka Berezovytsya, Ukraine

Gurukul Lutheran Theological College & Research Institute, Kilpauk, Chennai, India

Concordia Theological Seminary, Nagercoil, Tamil Nadu, India

Timothy Lutheran Seminary, Wabag Enga Province, Papua New Guinea

Martin Luther Seminary, Lae, Paupa New Guinea

Key to Abbreviations:

ELCA = Evangelical Lutheran Church in America

ELCIC = Evangelical Lutheran Church in Canada

LCC = Lutheran Church—Canada

LCMS = Lutheran Church—Missouri Synod

WELS = Wisconsin Evangelical Lutheran Synod

Source: Lutheran Education Conference of North America, www.lutherancolleges.org/collegelist.

ELCA CONGREGATIONS IN THE

Alaska Hawaii

Key
 = 1 congregation

UNITED STATES

Puerto Rico

Note: Congregations in the Bahamas and Virgin Islands are not shown. Congregational locations are approximate.
Sources: ELCA Congregation Report Forms, U.S. Census, Claritas
Prepared by ELCA Department For Research and Evaluation

GLOSSARY OF LUTHERAN WORSHIP TERMS

acolyte From the Greek for "to follow"; a lay liturgical assistant (often but not necessarily a youth) who serves in such various roles as crucifer, torchbearer, bannerbearer, bookbearer, candlelighter, and server.

Advent From the Latin for "coming"; the four weeks before Christmas which constitute the first season of the liturgical year.

Advent wreath A wreath with four candles, used during the four weeks of Advent.

Affirmation of Baptism Rite used for confirmation, reception of new members, and restoration to membership.

alb Full-length white vestment used in worship since the sixth century; usually worn with cincture. Worn by presiding and assisting ministers, acolytes, choristers.

altar Table in the chancel used for the celebration of the Holy Communion. It is the central furnishing of the worship space.

altar rail Railing enclosing the chancel at which people stand or kneel to receive Holy Communion.

ambo Another (more historic) name for the pulpit, reading desk, or lectern.

ante-communion That portion of the Holy Communion liturgy preceding the great thanksgiving.

antependium Parament for pulpit and lectern.

apse The semicircular (or polygonal) projection or alcove at the end of the chancel in traditional church architecture.

Ascension Principal festival occurring 40 days after Easter Day, celebrating Christ's ascension to heaven.

ashes Symbol of repentance and mortality used in the Ash Wednesday liturgy; made by burning palms from previous year.

Ash Wednesday First day of Lent; occurs between February 4 and March 10. Name derives from the traditional practice of imposing ashes on worshipers' foreheads.

assisting minister Lay person who assists the ordained presiding minister in worship leadership.

baptism The sacrament of water and the Holy Spirit, in which we are joined to Christ's death and resurrection and initiated into the church.

baptistery The area in which the baptismal font is located.

Benedicite, omnia opera (benn-eh-DEECH-ih-tay, OHM-nee-ah OH-purr-ah) Latin title for the final canticle in the Easter Vigil, "All you works of the Lord, bless the Lord," from Song of the Three Young Men.

Benedictus (benn-eh-DIK-tus) Latin title for the gospel canticle "Blessed be the God of Israel," in Morning Prayer, from Luke 1:68-79.

black Liturgical color for Ash Wednesday; symbolizes ashes, repentance, and humiliation.

blue Liturgical color for Advent; symbolizes hope.

burse Square fabric-covered case in which the communion linens are often carried to and from the altar.

candlelighter Long-handled device used to light and extinguish candles.

candlestick Ornamental base holder for candle.

cassock Full-length black "undergarment" worn under surplice or cotta.

catechumen A person (usually an adult or older youth) preparing for Holy Baptism through a process of formation and special rites leading up to baptism at the Easter Vigil.

catechumenate The process for preparing adults and older youth for Holy Baptism, often culminating at the Easter Vigil. It is a process of growth in spirituality, worship, service, as well as learning, and is based on the practice of the early church.

censer Vessel in which incense is burned; also called thurible.

chalice Cup used for the wine in the Holy Communion.

chancel Elevated area where altar and pulpit/ambo are located.

chasuble (CHAH-zuh-bel) The principal vestment for the Holy Communion liturgy; worn like a poncho by the presiding minister over alb and stole.

chrism (krizm) From the Greek for "Anointed One," a title for Christ. Fragrant oil used for anointing in Holy Baptism.

chrismon (KRIZ-mohn) From the words "Christ monograms"; symbols of Christ often used to decorate Christmas trees.

Christ the King The last Sunday of the church year, celebrating the kingship or sovereignty of Christ.

Christmas Principal festival of the church year which celebrates Christ's birth or nativity; also known as the Nativity of Our Lord.

ciborium (sih-BOR-ee-um) Tall covered vessel which holds wafers for the Holy Communion.

cincture (SINK-chur) Rope belt worn with an alb.

columbarium (KOLL-um-BARR-ee-um) Wall or other structure with niches for burial of ashes from cremation.

Compline (KAHM-plin) From the Latin for "complete," referring to the prayers which complete the day's worship. An order for night prayer used as the last worship service before bed. Also known as Prayer at the Close of the Day.

confirmation Liturgical form of Affirmation of Baptism, marking the completion of a period of instruction in the Christian faith. Used with youth who were baptized as infants.

cope Long cape worn by worship leader, lay or ordained, for certain processions and ceremonial occasions.

corporal Square white linen cloth placed on the center of the fair linen on the mensa, on which the eucharistic vessels are placed for the celebration of Holy Communion.

corpus Latin for "body." Carved figure of Christ attached to a cross; together, cross and corpus are a crucifix.

cotta (KOTT-ah) Short white vestment worn over cassock by acolytes and choir members (unless albs are worn).

credence (KREE-dentz) Shelf or table at chancel wall which holds sacramental vessels and offering plates.

crosier (KROH-zher) Crook-shaped staff often carried by a bishop in his/her own synod as a sign of shepherding authority.

crucifer The lay assisting minister or senior acolyte who carries the processional cross or crucifix.

crucifix Cross with a corpus attached.

cruet Glass vessel containing wine for the Holy Communion, oil for anointing, or water for the lavabo.

A cruet.

daily prayer The daily services of readings and prayer, including Morning Prayer (Matins), Evening Prayer (Vespers), and Night Prayer (Compline).

dossal Fabric hanging behind and above traditional east-wall altar.

east wall The wall behind the altar, regardless of whether the wall is geographically to the east.

eastwall altar An altar attached to the wall.

Easter Principal festival of the church year which celebrates Christ's resurrection. Easter Day (which occurs between March 22 and April 25) is known as the Resurrection of Our Lord and as the "queen of feasts." The Easter season lasts for 50 days, a "week of weeks."

Easter Vigil Festive liturgy on Easter Eve that includes the lighting of the new fire and procession of the paschal candle, readings from Scripture, Holy Baptism with the renewal of baptismal vows, and Holy Communion.

elements The earthly elements used in the celebration of the sacraments: bread and wine in Holy Communion, and water in Holy Baptism.

Epiphany Principal festival celebrated on January 6, marking the visit of the magi to Jesus and the consequent revelation of Christ to the world.

eucharist (YOO-kar-ist) From the Greek for "thanksgiving"; a name for the Holy Communion. The sacrament of Word, bread, and wine (in which the two earthly elements constitute the body and blood of our Lord) for which we give thanks, and through which we are nourished and strengthened in Christ's name and sustained in baptismal unity in him.

Fraction of the bread in Holy Communion.

Evening Prayer An evening worship service of scripture readings and prayer; also known as Vespers.

ewer (YOO-er) A pitcher used for carrying water to the baptismal font.

fair linen Top white linen cloth covering the mensa of the altar and thus serving as the table cloth for the Lord's Supper.

flagon (FLAG-un) Pitcher-like vessel from which wine is poured into the chalice for the Holy Communion.

font From the Latin for "fountain"; the pool or basin which holds water for Holy Baptism.

fraction Ceremonial breaking of the bread in the Holy Communion liturgy.

free-standing altar An altar which is not attached to the wall, and behind which the ministers stand (facing the congregation) for the celebration of Holy Communion.

frontal Parament that covers the entire front of the altar, from the top edge of the mensa down to the floor; *see also* Laudian frontal.

funeral pall Large white cloth cover placed on the coffin when brought into the nave for the burial liturgy. If an urn is used for ashes, a small white cloth is used to cover it.

gold Liturgical color for Easter Day, giving special prominence to this single most important festival of the year.

Good Friday The Friday in Holy Week that observes Christ's crucifixion and death. The chancel and altar are bare of all appointments, paraments, and linens.

Greek cross Ancient form of the cross in which the four arms are of equal length.

green Liturgical color for the nonfestival seasons after Pentecost and Epiphany; symbolic of growth in the Christian way of life.

Holy Trinity The First Sunday after Pentecost, which celebrates the doctrine of the Trinity (one God in three persons: Father, Son, and Holy Spirit).

Holy Week The week between the Sunday of the Passion (Palm Sunday) and Easter, which recalls the events of the last days of Christ's life.

host Wafer, made of unleavened bread, for the Holy Communion.

host box Short, round, covered container which holds the supply of hosts for the Holy Communion. Also known as pyx.

incense Mixture of resins for ceremonial burning, symbolic of our prayers rising to God (see Psalm 141); one of the gifts of the magi to Jesus on the Epiphany.

Incense.

intinction From the Latin for "to dip"; the practice of administering the eucharistic elements by dipping the host into the wine; does not work well with whole bread.

Laudian frontal A type of frontal which entirely covers the top and all sides (to the floor) of a free-standing altar.

lavabo bowl (lah-VAH-boh) Bowl used for the act of cleansing the presiding minister's hands (this act is known as the lavabo) in the Holy Communion or after the imposition of ashes or oil.

lectern Reading stand in the chancel from which the scripture readings may be proclaimed.

lectionary The appointed system of scripture readings for the days of the church year. Also refers to the book that contains these readings.

lector A lay assisting minister who reads the first and second readings from Scripture in the Holy Communion liturgy, or the biblical readings in other rites.

Lent From the Anglo-Saxon for "spring"; the penitential 40-day season (excluding Sundays) before Easter, beginning with Ash Wednesday. Symbolic of Christ's 40 days in the wilderness. Lent is traditionally the season when candidates prepare for Holy Baptism, which is celebrated at the Easter Vigil.

lenten veil Cloth used to cover crosses, sculpture, pictures, and other objects during Lent.

linens Refers to three groups of white linen cloths: altar linens (cerecloth, protector linen, and fair linen), communion linens (corporal, pall, purificators, and veil), and other linens (credence linen, offertory table linen, lavabo towel, and baptismal towel).

liturgy From the Greek for "the people's work"; the prescribed worship service of the church.

Magnificat (mahg-NIFF-ih-kaht) Latin title for the canticle, "My soul proclaims the greatness of the Lord," which is the gospel canticle in Evening Prayer, and is from Luke 1:46-55.

Matins (MAT-ins) From the Latin for "morning"; morning service of scripture reading and prayer; also known as Morning Prayer.

Maundy Thursday (MAWN-dee) From the Latin *mandatum* for "commandment"; the Thursday in Holy Week which commemorates the institution of the Holy Communion at the Last Supper, during which Jesus commanded his disciples to love one another.

memorial garden Usually a courtyard garden on church property in which ashes are mixed with the soil for interment after cremation.

mensa From the Latin for "table"; the top surface of the altar.

missal Altar service book.

missal stand Stand or cushion on the altar on which the altar service book is placed during the Holy Communion liturgy.

miter (MY-ter) From the Greek for "turban." A liturgical hat worn by a bishop.

Morning Prayer Morning service of scripture reading and prayer; also known as Matins.

narthex Entrance hall and gathering space of a church building which leads to the nave.

nave From the Latin for "ship"; the section of the church building between the narthex and the chancel, where the congregation assembles for worship.

new fire The fire kindled on Easter Eve, used to light the paschal candle for the Easter Vigil. Symbolic of Christ's resurrected presence.

Nunc dimittis (NOONK dih-MIH-tiss) Latin title for the canticle from Luke 2:29-32, "Now, Lord, you let your servant go in peace," used in Night Prayer and as a song after Holy Communion.

occasional service Liturgical rite used from time to time, including rites for burial, marriage, healing, ordination, dedication of a church building, installation of a pastor, confirmation (Affirmation of Baptism), and so forth.

ordinary Those parts of the eucharistic liturgy which do not change from week to week.

Miters go on top of bishops. They've been wearing them a long time.

orphrey (OR-free) From the Latin for "gold." Ornamental band on a chasuble or parament.

ossuary Small container holding the remains after a cremation.

pall Linen-covered square placed over rim of the chalice. (*See also* funeral pall.)

Palm Sunday *See* Sunday of the Passion.

paraments Cloth hangings of various seasonal liturgical colors used to adorn the altar and pulpit/ambo/lectern.

paschal candle Large white candle carried in procession during the Easter Vigil, placed near the altar and lighted during the Easter season, symbolizing Christ's resurrected presence. At other times of the year, it is placed near the font and lighted for Holy Baptism, and placed at the head of the coffin and lighted for the burial liturgy.

Paschal candle.

paten (PATT-en) Plate used to hold bread or hosts during the Holy Communion liturgy.

pectoral cross A cross on a chain, worn around the neck by a bishop.

Pentecost From the Greek for "fiftieth day"; principal festival of the church year, occurring 50 days after Easter. Celebrates the descent of the Holy Spirit to the crowd gathered in Jerusalem.

Phos hilaron (FOHS HILL-uh-ron) Greek for "light of glory"; hence, the Greek name for the canticle in Evening Prayer which begins "Joyous light of glory."

piscina A special drain in the sacristy which goes directly into the ground, used for disposal of baptismal water and wine remaining in the chalice after the Holy Communion.

Prayer at the Close of the Day Night prayer service used as the last worship before retiring for the night. Also known as Compline or Night Prayer.

presiding minister The ordained pastor who presides at a worship service.

Processional Cross.

prie-dieu (pree-DYOO) French term for "prayer desk"; used in the chancel for daily prayer services, confirmation, and weddings, as well as by ministers at other times when kneeling for prayer is desired.

processional cross A cross or crucifix on a tall staff used to lead processions.

processional torch *See* torch.

propers The varying portions of the communion service which are appointed for each day (or season) of the church year; include the prayer of the day, psalm, readings, gospel acclamation, and proper preface.

protector linen White linen cloth placed on the mensa between the cerecloth and the fair linen, to which the parament may be attached.

pulpit Raised reading desk in the chancel from which the gospel is read and the sermon preached. *See also* ambo.

purificator Square linen napkin used to cleanse the rim of the chalice during the distribution of Holy Communion.

purple Liturgical color for Lent, symbolizing penitence.

pyx (PIKS) *See* host box.

red Bright red liturgical color, symbolic of the fire of the Holy Spirit. Used on the Day of Pentecost, Reformation Day, martyrs' days, and on major church occasions such as ordination, the dedication of a church building, church anniversaries, and synod/churchwide assemblies.

reredos (RAIR-eh-doss) Carved stone or wood panel behind and above an eastwall altar.

Responsive Prayer Brief liturgical order of versicles and responses.

retable (REE-tay-bel) A step or shelf at the rear of the mensa of an eastwall altar, on which cross, candlesticks, and flowers are placed. Also known as a gradine.

rite The text and ceremonies of a liturgical worship service.

rubric From the Latin for "red"; a direction for the proper conduct of a worship service. Rubrics are usually printed in red.

sacrament A rite commanded by Christ that uses an earthly element with the word of God to convey God's grace; Holy Baptism and Holy Communion.

sacristy A room used for storage and preparation of items needed in worship; also used for vesting before services.

sanctuary The section of the chancel that immediately surrounds the altar.

sanctuary lamp A constantly burning candle sometimes suspended from the ceiling or mounted on the chancel wall; in Roman Catholic and some Episcopal churches, symbolizes the reserved sacrament.

Sanctuary lamp, bronze hanging.

scarlet The deep red liturgical color used from the Sunday of the Passion (Palm Sunday) through Maundy Thursday. Symbolic of the blood of the passion of Christ.

sign of the cross Gesture of tracing the outline of the cross with the hand, as a mark of belonging to Christ in Holy Baptism (during which it is first placed on one's forehead).

spoon Perforated utensil sometimes used to remove foreign particles from wine in the chalice. A spoon is also used with the granular incense.

stole Cloth band in liturgical color worn over the alb or surplice around a pastor's neck and hanging to the knees. Signifies ordination and the yoke of obedience to Christ.

stripping of the altar Ceremony at the conclusion of the Maundy Thursday liturgy, in which all appointments, linens, and paraments are removed from the altar and chancel in preparation for Good Friday.

Sunday of the Passion The first day of Holy Week, also known as Palm Sunday. Commemorates both Christ's triumphant entry into Jerusalem and his crucifixion.

superfrontal Short parament that hangs over the front of the mensa of an eastwall altar; now rarely used.

surplice White vestment worn over the cassock; used especially for daily prayer services.

Te Deum laudamus (tay DAY-um lau-DAH-moos) Latin for "We praise you, God"; a title for the canticle used in Morning Prayer.

Tenebrae (TENN-eh-bray) From the Latin for "shadows"; a service sometimes used evenings during Holy Week, in which candles on a Tenebrae candle hearse are gradually extinguished.

Torch.

thurible Vessel in which incense is burned; also known as a censer.

thurifer The person who carries the thurible.

torch Large candle on a staff carried in processions, often flanking the processional cross or gospel book.

torchbearer An acolyte who carries a processional torch.

Transfiguration Festival celebrated on the last Sunday after the Epiphany, recalling Christ's transfiguration on the mountain.

Triduum (TRIH-doo-um) Latin for "three days"; the three sacred days from Maundy Thursday evening through Easter Evening, which together celebrate the unity of the paschal mystery of Christ's death and resurrection.

urn *see* ossuary.

veil Cloth placed over sacramental vessels before and after the celebration of Holy Communion.

versicles Brief lines of scripture (often from the psalms) sung or said responsively in certain rites, including daily prayer.

Vespers From the Latin for "evening"; an evening worship service of scripture readings and prayer. Also known as Evening Prayer.

vigil A liturgical service on the eve of a festival, such as the Easter Vigil.

white Liturgical color used on festivals of Christ, the weeks of Christmas and Easter, The Holy Trinity, and certain saints' days. Symbolizes joy, gladness, purity, and the light of Christ.

EVERYDAY STUFF

HOW TO RECEIVE GOD'S GRACE DAILY

God's grace exists in a dual, paradoxical state that many Protestant theologians describe as being *transcendent and immanent*—that is, above and beyond the realm of human understanding, but also ever-present and constantly available to human beings. One suggested analogy involves the human as a radio, "tuned in" to God's grace the same way a dial is set to a constant, pre-existing signal.

 Don't do anything.
Receiving God's grace doesn't depend on what you do or how much you believe. Grace can be received only as a free gift from God through Jesus Christ.

 Avoid frantic seeking, searching, or striving.
The word *receive* implies a key stance of passivity befitting the recipient of a gift. Grace is a revealed gift; it cannot be commanded, controlled, or earned.

 Stay positive.
Certain attitudes of the recipient make grace easier to recognize. These include: thankfulness, obedience, and not being invested in the outcome of situations. It can, in part, be described by this phrase from the Lord's Prayer: "Your will be done."

④ Remain spiritually still; practice stillness in all its forms.
Grace, coming from God, is often received and perceived in quiet moments that allow the "still small voice" of God to speak a peace that passes understanding.

*God's grace has been compared to a kind of omnipresent,
ever-present radio signal to which human beings can be tuned.*

5 Utilize prayer as a means to tune your dial to the
right signal.

Meditative prayer is often best, as it encourages the
values mentioned above, but the beloved Serenity Prayer
is a viable linguistic means: "God grant me the serenity

to accept the things I cannot change; courage to change the things I can; and wisdom to know the difference."

Be Aware

- For Lutherans, God's grace is both *hidden* and *revealed* at the same time.
- God's grace is clearly *visible*, however, in the life, death, and resurrection of Jesus Christ. For confirmation of God's love for you, direct your attention to the cross.
- Receiving God's grace is not contingent on the results of a pass-fail behavior test.
- The Rev. James Jones, Bishop of Liverpool, explains grace thusly: "The best thing about grace is that God loves you just as you are. That is truly wonderful, that is good news for any human being on the face of this planet."

HOW TO PROCLAIM THE GOSPEL TO SOMEONE WHO NEEDS TO HEAR IT

Christian belief puts overwhelming stress on the Word and preaching the gospel to others through a verbal declaration. For Lutherans, this declaration is the thing sinners afflicted by the law hunger and wait and listen for; learning how to declare it in life situations, therefore, is a critical skill that requires both practice and boldness.

❶ Assess the human need at hand.
Is the person hungry? Lonely? Depressed? Diseased? Spiritual needs can become manifest through physical, behavioral or psychological symptoms. Most often the affliction is the result of some law or other having remorselessly gone to work on the person.

❷ Avoid neglecting the physical opportunities to bring the gospel.
Although he delivered many sermons and teachings and was himself God's forgiveness and salvation for sinners, Christ's ministry was physically dynamic: he washed feet, cleansed lepers, healed the sick, and raised the dead. When such physical acts accompany an authentic delivery of the gospel, the impact is more than double.

❸ Remain humble. Avoid foisting.
Preaching the gospel in one-on-one situations is a holy moment in which God is at work. Assume a self-effacing but firm stance, which is likely to result in an open, inviting listener. Use direct, true, conversational language. Syrupy, over-the-top, disingenuous Jesus-talk is likely to ring hollow to skeptical listeners, especially hard-bitten Lutherans.

The gospel is usually best proclaimed in words aimed directly at another person's situation in which freedom in Jesus Christ and liberation from sin are particularly needed.

❹ **Declare the gospel aloud and without reservation.**
Say, "The devil assaults you with this law because he knows Christ lives in you through your baptism. Jesus died on the cross to put that devil under his foot and raise you up into a new life. You are forgiven." Or something along those lines.

❺ **Follow through.**
Just as Christ built a relationship with you, try maintaining a relationship with those to whom you declare the gospel whenever possible. Multiple declarations will probably be required, especially to those unfamiliar with the language of faith.

Be Aware

- Sinners also need to hear the law, but clearly defined. Proclamation of the gospel is most effective when preceded by clarification that names the Old Adam or Old Eve in them.
- Blanket proclamations of judgment, hellfire, condemnation, along with scriptural citations, shaming, or using the voice and cadence of a televangelist (particularly by drawing out the name *Jeeee-sus*) will almost always achieve a negative result.

The gospel can be preached in deed as well in the form of physical acts of kindness that speak where words alone might not suffice.

THE TOP THREE USES OF THE LAW

"You shall have no other gods." That's the First Commandment. There are more than 600 additional commands in the first five books of the Old Testament. Additionally, there are dozens of rules in the New Testament, such as Jesus' request, "Just as I have loved you, you also should love one another" (John 13:34), and "pray without ceasing" (1 Thessalonians 5:17). Lutherans have always understood that the law has particular functions, also called "uses."

❶ The first use of the law.
Latin term: *usus civilis* ("civil use").

At face value, laws simply let us know what is required of us in terms of conduct. The law, therefore, is first given in order to maintain discipline so our sinful impulses are kept in check, order is maintained, and human community can be possible.

The first use of the law is to restrain sin and evil and keep good order.

❷ The second use of the law.
Latin term: *Usus pedegogicus* ("pedagogical use").

The law *teaches* us (a) that we always fall short of keeping it, (b) that we are sinners, and (c) that we need someone to save us from sin and its consequences. That is, the law's second use drives us to Christ and his cross. For Lutherans this use is the most important use because it leads to salvation.

❸ The third use of the law.
Latin term: *usus tertius* ("third use").

Most Lutherans believe that after one becomes a Christian, the law is still necessary. "Third Users" believe that apart from the first use a third use must be applied in order to establish a Christian pattern of life. "Non-Third Users" argue that the third use is redundant and unnecessary, saying the first use gives Christians all they need in this regard.

Like a tough teacher, the second use of the law truthfully instructs us as to our sinful nature and drives us always toward Jesus Christ who is our salvation.

Be Aware

- Lutherans generally agree about the first two uses of the law. The third use has been a bone of contention, however. In 1580, a group of second-generation Lutherans attempted to reach a concord on the issue, but the issue persists even today.
- There are only three known uses of the law. There is no fourth or fifth use. Also no sixth use. Some archeologists thought they had uncovered a seventh use once, but they hadn't. No seventh use, either.

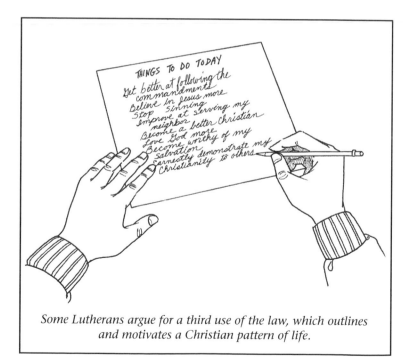

Some Lutherans argue for a third use of the law, which outlines and motivates a Christian pattern of life.

HOW TO HEAP GRACE ON YOUR ENEMIES' HEADS LIKE HOT COALS

It is said that by doing good to one's enemies one will heap burning coals on their heads. It is often overlooked that the source for this mandate, Romans 12:19-21, concludes, "Do not be overcome by evil, but overcome evil with good." Only gracious kindness can overcome anger and the desire for revenge, and true kindness is never malicious or destructive.

❶ Keep in mind that you and your enemies are intimately connected.
What diminishes or hurts one of you diminishes and hurts all the others. Your own self-interest is the same as their self-interests.

❷ Resign from anger. Train your heart to see your enemies as teachers and partners in your life.
Make the spiritual commitment to give up regarding those who mean or do you harm as objects of hatred or revenge. Only when you can see them objectively and dispassionately will you be able to break the cycle of anger and become a source of grace to them.

❸ Buy your enemy a gift certificate for a massage.
Make your enemy's physical well-being a matter of great concern. When more relaxed, an enemy may be kinder to others than they have been to you.

4 Treat your enemies' children with fawning respect.
It is possible to break a cycle of enmity by showing
regard for the things and people your enemies care
most about because this boldly illustrates your
interconnectedness. Congratulate their kids on their
accomplishments and send them copies of newspaper
articles that mention them.

5 Pray for your enemies' health.
Avoid delighting in his or her misfortune and ailments;
pray for your enemy as though for yourself or someone
you love.

6 Speak well of your enemies even when others do not
(Eighth Commandment).
Remain consistent in your thoughts and remarks, and
put the best possible construction on your enemies'
actions and behavior.

Be Aware

- People who allow themselves to be shaped by the love
of Christ and do as he commands in this regard will
naturally attract fewer and fewer enemies and more and
more friends.
- Missteps are inevitable, which is where forgiveness
comes in.

Placing a premium on your enemy's health and well-being by buying him or her a shiatsu, hot stone, or deep-muscle massage can put you in the right frame of mind and heap burning coals of grace on his or her head, metaphorically speaking.

HOW TO TELL THE DIFFERENCE BETWEEN CHEAP GRACE AND REGULAR GRACE

The Lutheran understanding of grace is often summed up by Ephesians 2:8-9, "For by grace you have been saved through faith, and this is not your own doing; it is the gift of God— not the result of works, so that no one may boast." The term "cheap grace" applies when a person knowingly uses God's grace as a justification for sin—by commission or omission. The following rationales usually signal the presence of cheap grace:

❶ "I know God will forgive me, so I'm going to _____ anyway."

No sin is unforgivable. However, as Paul writes in Romans 2:4, "Do you realize that God's kindness is meant to lead us to repentance?"

❷ "Jesus threw out the old law and made a new law."

Jesus conquered sin, death, and the power of the devil when he died and rose again. However, the law still applies. Jesus addressed this in his Sermon on the Mount when he said, "Do not think that I have come to abolish the law or the prophets; I have come not to abolish but to fulfill" (Matthew 5:17).

❸ "It's easier to ask for forgiveness than permission."

If so, you're probably looking for a helping of cheap grace. Isaiah 66:2 says God looks to the "humble and contrite in spirit." God doesn't call us to go through the motions of asking forgiveness as a formality. People aren't truly "contrite" if they knew in advance they were about to do something wrong.

Regular grace is actually quite costly, as it has been paid for through Jesus' precious blood and innocent suffering and death in atonement for our sins. Regular grace is a free gift to you.

❹ "Sin boldly."

Many well-meaning Lutherans invoke this partial quote by Martin Luther to justify their sins. In fact, Luther intended to refute cheap grace when he said, "Sin boldly, but believe and rejoice in Christ even more boldly, for he is victorious over sin, death, and the world." Your identity in Christ is the critical thing; glossing over sin with half-truths only obscures this.

Be Aware

- Humans manufacture cheap grace. Regular grace pops out of nowhere, undeserved, uncontrived, and dismantles all your self-justifications before Christ because it comes straight from God.
- Paul reminds us in Romans 6:1-2, "What then are we to say? Should we continue in sin in order that grace may abound? By no means! How can we who died to sin go on living in it?"
- *Antinomian* is a fancy word for someone who indulges in "cheap grace." (Anti = "against," Nomian = "law.")

Cheap grace is most often attended by a certain flip attitude and used as excuse or permission for sin. Cheap grace is manufactured by humans and costs nothing.

HOW TO REPENT

Christians regard repentance as a fundamental benefit of the Christian life. Jesus said, "The kingdom of God is near. Repent and believe the good news" (Mark 1:15). The New Testament word for repent means "to change one's mind," as in to change one's heart and life completely. The Old Testament word for repent means "to turn," as in to turn away from sin and back to God.

Repentance is about turning away from sin and turning back toward God. God calls us to repent both "once" in our lives and also "every day." Those who don't know the Lord repent "once"—to turn toward the Lord and be saved by God's grace. Those who already know the Lord repent "every day"—to turn away from the evil and sin that tempts us, and turn back to God. In both cases, the method of repentance is the same.

❶ **Hear God's Word.**
God's Word instructs us about the sin in our lives. The Word shows us those things about us that are not of God. God's Word comes to us through Jesus, through the Scriptures, and through preaching.

❷ **Recognize and admit your sin.**
Part of repentance is acknowledging our sin and being sorry for the wrong we do: "Godly sorrow brings repentance" (2 Corinthians 7:10). Tell God you know you sin and that you are sorry for your sin.

❸ **Ask the Holy Spirit for help turning back to God.**
A person cannot repent or turn to God on his or her own. Ask God for help. Pray in the name of Jesus that the Holy Spirit would come to you and turn you back to the Lord.

❹ Live as a forgiven sinner.
God wants us to live in the way that is best for us and best for our neighbors—a way that points to God. Live according to God's will, loving God and your neighbor with all your heart.

❺ Repeat the process daily.
Repentance is a way of life. Every day brings new opportunities to hear God's Word, acknowledge and be sorry for the wrong we do, ask God for help, and live as forgiven sinners.

Be Aware

• In cases when no particular sin can be called to mind, repentance should nonetheless be undertaken earnestly. Simply tell God that you are sorry for sins you are not aware of. You have certainly committed some.

HOW TO IDENTIFY A "NEIGHBOR" AND WHAT THIS MEANS FOR LUTHERANS

Luther's "neighbor" theology was firmly rooted in his belief in Jesus Christ, who came not to be served but to serve. Luther professed that as followers of Christ, each of us is called to be a "little Christ" to others. These "others" are our neighbors, whom God places in our lives on purpose. Important earmarks for recognizing a neighbor may include the following:

❶ Look for obvious signs of being in need.
If you see someone in need, assume that person is a neighbor. Signs of need include hunger, lack of shelter, distress or anxiety, or destructive behavior patterns. People with poor fashion sense are neighbors but may require a lighter touch.

❷ Apply a reckless lack of discrimination in your analysis.
Jesus ate with tax collectors and prostitutes. There is no universal profile for identifying a neighbor. Neighbors come in all shapes, sizes, colors, and ages and are often people you would least like to have as your neighbors. *Note:* Suffering unneighborly behavior from someone does not exempt you from regarding that person as a neighbor.

❸ Practice receiving others' neighborliness with grace.
Your own skills in identifying and serving your neighbor may improve as you focus on the extraordinary kindnesses you receive daily from those around you. Adopt an attitude of abundance in this regard.

④ Make a thorough inventory of all neighbors within your personal reach.
Family members, roommates, coworkers, bad drivers, children, and convenience store clerks should be included in your list. Practice Christlike neighborliness toward these people.

⑤ Consider expanding your neighborly sphere of influence.
The Internet has opened and expanded opportunities to recognize neighbors around the world and to serve them. Be vigilant in serving distant neighbors. Support global missions or world hunger programs to meet their needs.

⑥ Define "neighbor" as liberally as possible.
Strive to abandon stereotypes and to embrace the unfamiliar and weird. We cannot limit who we call "neighbor." God's love excludes no one.

Be Aware

* Being a good neighbor can include actions other than sheer kindness.
* Focusing efforts regularly on defining yourself can help you become a better neighbor to others.

HOW TO ADOPT AN EVANGELISTIC LIFESTYLE WITHOUT ALIENATING PEOPLE

Some Christians believe adopting an evangelistic lifestyle means they must seek to drag people to church, a tactic that can backfire when applied injudiciously. Adopting an evangelistic lifestyle simply means living a life that reflects that the teachings of Jesus are active in your mind and heart.

❶ Adopt an attitude of welcoming, personal hospitality, and acceptance.
Jesus invited people of little status to join him wherever he was. He dined with sinners, tax collectors, and women—people who often were disregarded during biblical times. Follow Jesus' example.

❷ Actively seek out opportunities to serve as Jesus did.
When you live an evangelistic lifestyle, you actively look for ways to serve the needs of others and to treat all people as neighbors.

❸ Initiate natural and unforced faith conversations as a matter of habit.
Talk about your faith journey and where it has led you. Compare notes with others without casting judgment. Avoid falling in love with the sound of your own voice or the repeated retelling of your life story. Attempt to learn something from everyone.

Unpretentiousness is a valuable ally when attempting to adopt an evangelistic lifestyle. Act casually.

④ Consider wearing symbols of your faith; avoid contrived garishness.

Wear a tasteful cross necklace on a regular basis, but consider concealing it from time to time under clothing. Read the Bible during your lunch hour, but consider purchasing an edition with an unobtrusive cover. Displaying faith symbols offers others the opportunity to ask about them, but glaring announcements of Jesus loving can have an undesirable effect.

⑤ Establish a habit of wanton forgiveness.
Everybody makes mistakes. Make forgiveness a foundation of your life. Forgiveness consumes less energy than anger or revenge, and it serves as a strong witness to God's work.

⑥ Maintain a rigorous prayer schedule.
An important foundation for an evangelistic lifestyle is regular conversations with God, which centers you for daily living.

Be Aware

- Many people may have experienced "evangelistic" people as unnecessarily negative and judgmental. Use grace and forgiveness to counteract this negativism.
- How you act may be more important than what you say.

HOW TO TITHE

The Old Testament contains many references to tithing as the giving standard for God's people. A "tithe" (10th) is simply 10 percent of one's income given directly to fund God's work. Tithing requires a conscious decision, discipline, and sacrifice and may take a lifetime to achieve, but seasoned tithers report extraordinary spiritual dividends.

❶ Commit to the goal of giving 10 percent, come what may.
Tithing requires fortitude and perseverance. Resolve not to waver; consider sealing your commitment with a ceremonial "first check" or a tattoo.

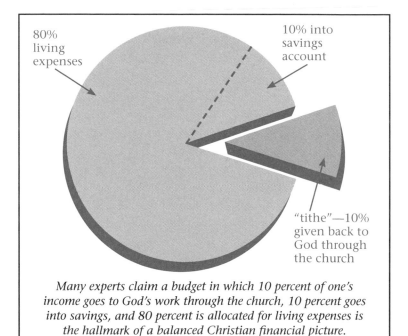

80%
living
expenses

10% into
savings
account

"tithe"—10%
given back to
God through
the church

Many experts claim a budget in which 10 percent of one's income goes to God's work through the church, 10 percent goes into savings, and 80 percent is allocated for living expenses is the hallmark of a balanced Christian financial picture.

❷ Make a sound financial plan.

Develop a three-to-five-year plan to achieve tithing, and break up the years with meaningful milestones, such as, "5 percent by year two!" Consider three steps that will get you to 10 percent. For longer-term plans, increase your giving by 1 percent of your income each year until you reach 10 percent. Tithing should have an impact on your household budget, but it should not bankrupt you.

❸ Establish your tithing channels.

Many tithers give all 10 percent to their home congregation, while others divide it among charities and service organizations that are close to their hearts. Remember that properly placed tithes to reputable organizations are tax-deductible; you'll receive a statement in January of each year. Many congregations send quarterly statements to help keep members on track.

❹ Consider multiple methods of accountability to help you stay focused.

Talk with other members of your congregation about tithing. Making the journey to tithing together can help make it an achievable and meaningful discipline. Consider asking your pastor to pray for your tithing plan.

Be Aware

- While tithing can be extremely difficult at times, experienced tithers claim the difficult moments are in fact spiritual challenges that have deepened their faith and trust in God.
- Spread the word about tithing quietly with a positive message. If every member of your congregation became a tither, your church could invest heavily in real estate.
- Avoid bragging, boasting, or making others feel inferior when tithing.
- Like tattoos or soap operas, tithing can be habit forming. Most Christians maintain they have never known an ex-tither.

SEVEN COMPLICATED LUTHERAN THEOLOGICAL TERMS IN LATIN AND WHAT THEY MEAN IN PLAIN ENGLISH

Lutheran theologians like to throw around Latin phrases as they argue the finer points of the original "evangelical" theology. This is partly because Latin was the official language of Luther's day and all scholarly writing was done in Latin, and partly because theologians like to sound smarter than you. Memorize the following phrases to impress or alienate your friends.

1 *Facere quod in se est* (fack-array kwahd in say est), "Do your best."
This is the theological saying that caused Luther so much despair when he was a young monk. If you had to "do your best" in order for God to meet you halfway with grace, Luther wanted to know how could you possibly know when you'd done enough?

2 *Justitia Dei* (yuss-titee-ah day-ee), "God's righteousness."
Lutherans believe God *makes* people righteous by grace, through faith, on account of Christ (as revealed in Scripture) as pure gift. This is in contrast to the common idea that you have to exercise some righteousness yourself to earn the gift, whether by being a good person, or making decisions for Jesus, or going to church, or being really sincere, and so on.

❸ *Theologia crucis* (tay-oh-loh-gee-ah krew-kiss), "Theology of the Cross."
Luther wrote, "A theologian of glory calls evil good and good evil. A theologian of the cross calls a thing what it actually is." In the end, however, *theologia cruces* hinges on the idea that through the cross, "the Love of God does not find, but creates, that which is pleasing to God."

❹ *Servum arbitrium* (sair-womb ahr-bee-tree-uhm), "Bondage of the Will."
Because of the Fall (original sin) humans are *bound* to reject God's salvation in Christ. God, however, chooses to save rebellious sinners and overrides their will, as it were, making believers out of them. On this point, Luther once confessed that, "God has taken my salvation out of my hands and into his, making it depend on his choice and not mine, and has promised to save me, not by my own work or exertion but by his grace and mercy."

❺ *Libertate Christiani* (lee-bair-tah-tay kriss-tee-ahn-nee), "Freedom of a Christian."
Lutherans like "two-handed thinking" (on the one hand; on the other hand). Luther once wrote that "a Christian is a perfectly free Master, subject to no one," but then in the very next sentence, he wrote, "a Christian is a perfectly dutiful servant, subject to everyone." The point is, both statements are equally true and must be kept in balance.

❻ *Simul iustus et peccator* (see-muhl ee-you-stuss et pee-kah-tor), "Saint and Sinner at the same time."
On the one hand, there's the Old You, descended from Adam and Eve, separated from God, rebellious, sinful, cursed, and dying. On the other hand, there's the New You, born of water and the Word, joined to Christ, faithful, righteous, blessed, living now and forever. It's the split personality that began when you were baptized, the one Paul writes about in Romans, chapters 5–8.

7 *Lex et evangelium* (leks et ay-van-gay-lee-um), "Law and Gospel."
There's one phrase that sums it all up for Lutherans: *Lex et Evangelium.* For Lutherans, all of God's word can be discerned in terms of command or promise, or Law and Gospel. For Lutherans, to be a good theologian means being able to tell the difference between Law and Gospel, and speak the Word accordingly.

Honorable mentions include the following:

- *Adiaphora* (ah-dee-ah-fore-ah), **"Indifferent things."** This term refers to the Lutheran idea that one is free to adopt or not adopt nonessential, that is, human traditions. That includes the tradition of using Latin in theological discussion.
- *Deus absconditus; Deus revelatus* (day-oose ahb-skahn-dee-toose; day-oose ray-vay-lah-toose), **"The hidden God"; "The revealed God."** These terms refer to God's exceptional talent at playing hide-and-go-seek.
- *Solus Christus* (soh-loose kree-stoose), **"Christ alone."** Collectively known as "the solas," the three terms below reveal Luther's emphasis on each concept as an integrated whole, but together they constitute a pattern of theological thinking that transformed the world.
  Sola gratia (soh-lah grah-tee-ah), **"Grace alone."**
  Sola fide (soh-lah fee-day), **"Faith alone."**
  Sola scriptura (soh-lah skreep-too-rah), **"Scripture alone."**

Be Aware

- One is *not* required to know Latin to be a Lutheran.
- Using Latin terms in regular conversation may label you as a geek and diminish your chances of ever getting a date or having friends.

HOW TO TELL THE DIFFERENCE BETWEEN A "VOCATION" AND A "VACATION"

Martin Luther's doctrine of vocation is radical because Luther says that a holy *calling* (which is what the word *vocation* means) is not limited to people who are pastors or missionaries. Rather, any job or career is holy when a Christian performs it as part of her or his baptismal call from God to serve others.

A vacation.

❶ Consider the role of money in the context of the activity.

If someone is paying you (however little) rather than making you pay for the opportunity to do the activity, you may be living a vocation, rather than being on vacation.

❷ Assess the measure and type of fatigue that results from the activity.

If you are working very hard and getting very tired, but you are not exhausted or downcast, you may be living a vocation rather than being on a vacation. This is a point where vocation and vacation may overlap; discern carefully.

A vocation.

Vacations and vocations are quite different, as one is recreational and the other is "re-creational"—a life lived through the promises of baptism to participate in God's ongoing work of blessing and redeeming all creation.

❸ Check nearby tables for beverages with little umbrellas in them.

If you are serving others rather than being served by others, you may be living a vocation rather than being on vacation. Most employers do not cater to their employees with beverage cart service to their cubicles.

❹ Discern your impact on the people around you.

If people are genuinely grateful for your presence, rather than just saying so to get a bigger tip, you may be living a vocation rather than being on vacation.

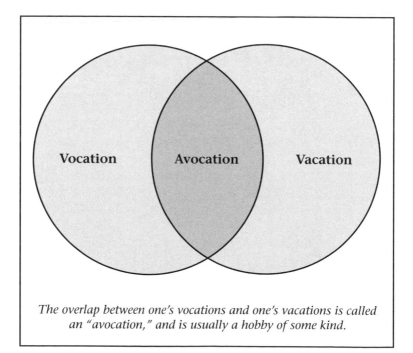

The overlap between one's vocations and one's vacations is called an "avocation," and is usually a hobby of some kind.

❺ Measure the level of challenge you experience during the activity.
  If challenged at multiple levels—intellectual, emotional, physical, and spiritual—by what you do each day, you may be living a vocation, rather than being on vacation. While hiking or surfing may be challenging in a physical way, hiking and surfing are probably not vocations for most people.

❻ Differentiate between your level of fulfillment and your level of relaxation.
  If you find fulfillment in what you do beyond mere relaxation and enjoyment, you may be living a vocation, rather than being on vacation.

Be Aware

- The Lutheran doctrine of vocation encompasses careers and roles outside of workplace employment. Father, mother, sister, brother, friend, and colleague are just a few of the vocations to which Christians are called.
- Vocations of the paid, workplace variety can change. God may choose to call you into many different vocations of this kind during your lifespan.
- Discerning to which vocations God is calling you is among the most important—and ongoing—challenges you face as a Christian.
- The overlap region between vocation and vacation is typically called an *avocation*, which means "a hobby or minor vocation." Avocations show many characteristics of both vocation and vacation, but they have their own name so folks should use it.

HOW TO TELL THE DIFFERENCE BETWEEN JUSTICE AND CHARITY

In the Bible, Jesus is most harsh with people who show no concern for those who are hungry, thirsty, without clothes, in prison, and sick. He tells his disciples, "Truly I tell you, just as you did not do it to one of the least of these, you did not do it to me" (Matthew 25:45). Charity and justice are two sides of the same coin—they go together, but they are distinct from each other.

❶ Charity typically includes personal interaction that results in relief.
In the parable of the good Samaritan, the Samaritan provided temporary and immediate relief to someone who was in need. Jesus said, "Go and do likewise" (Luke 10:29-37).

❷ Justice usually relates to acts that address unfair social, economic, or political systems.
Moses did not ask Pharaoh for food or supplies for his people, though they certainly needed them. Instead, Moses challenged the oppressive system that imposed suffering and slave labor upon his people. Moses went to the Pharaoh and said, "Let my people go" (Exodus 7:16).

❸ Apply a distinction of *emphasis*.
Moses focused on the long-term need of his people rather than the immediate and pressing needs for food and medicine. The good Samaritan's emphasis on charity was on the immediate relief of suffering. Moses' emphasis on justice was directed at the root cause of social injustice. While charity addresses the *symptoms* that are the result of poverty, justice addresses the *systems* that lead to poverty.

❹ Focus on charity in your daily and weekly life.
In your local congregation, working at a food bank in your community or volunteering at the local women's shelter is an important work of charity and an important aspect of a Christ-centered life.

❺ Connect your experiences of charity with a wider perspective.
Find ways to contribute to the elimination of structures that lead to hunger, poverty, or injustice. Consider becoming involved in legislative advocacy, or congregation-based community organizing as a way to address the systems that lead to such oppression.

Be Aware

- Lutherans tend toward excellence in charity but sometimes slow down a bit when it comes to justice, perhaps because they're uncomfortable being people who rock the boat. This is neither historically nor theologically necessary, as justice is a rudiment to the Lutheran heritage.
- Talk to your pastor or social concerns committee about the important connection and difference between charity and justice. Then find ways in your local congregation to get involved in both.

HOW TO TELL THE DIFFERENCE BETWEEN THEOLOGY OF THE CROSS AND THEOLOGY OF GLORY

Distinguishing between cross and glory theologies requires a keen mind and the ability to differentiate between law and gospel. Like other Lutheran concepts, this one is difficult to quantify because it is actually a *way of thinking* rather than a strict set of rules. Luckily, the learning curve is quite short due to the abundance of theology of glory in our world and culture.

❶ Pay extremely close attention to the use of language.
Lutherans are famous for overparsing other people's sentence structure, but this arises from a valuable theological instinct. Who is the actor in this case? What did they do? How was their action described? Who benefits? Who receives the glory for it? While these questions all sound like political suspicion they're actually a right-headed effort to expose theology of glory and keep the focus on Christ.

❷ Remain vigilant against the implication that human beings are all-powerful, especially with respect to their own salvation from sin and death.
Theologians of glory vastly overestimate a person's innate ability to believe and do the things necessary to gain access to God's grace—access that only God, through Jesus Christ, can grant. While perhaps not always consciously, they conceive of their own will as primary and God's as peripheral. They love sentences that begin with the pronoun "I."*

❸ Train your mind to favor God over human beings as the "subject of the sentence."

The theology of the cross claims the cross of Christ as a complete break from human "religious" efforts. That is, the cross represents *God's* decision and work for humans apart from any human action. Theologies of glory, on the other hand, nearly always emphasize human decision or work. Put simply, a theology of glory puts you in the driver's seat while a theology of the cross confesses that God does it all through the cross.

❹ Use the chart on the next page as a means of orienting your mind toward distinguishing the two theologies.

Be Aware

- Once you start looking for theologies of glory you begin to see them everywhere. One excellent example is in the movie *Indiana Jones and The Last Crusade* (1989). In the climactic scene, Indy must solve a series of booby-trapped puzzles to reach the Holy Grail. Before he can obtain the "Cup of the Carpenter" he has to "prove his worth" by (1) bowing in penance, (2) following in the footsteps of God's proper name, (3) taking a leap of faith, and (4) selecting the true grail from dozens of false ones. This represents a typical theology of glory: God's salvation—in this case, the healing cup—can only be attained by proper human decision and effort.
- When you relapse into theology of glory, as everyone does occasionally, avoid punishing yourself. Simply recognize it, go back, and start again.
- Luckily, it is not our theologies that save us, but Jesus Christ.

* Many theologians of glory become experts at camouflaging this move by confusing the words "I" and "God." In other words, beginning sentences with the word "God" does not *necessarily* make the statement one of theology of the cross. For example, "God told me to hit my sister," could be used to cloak unsavory ulterior motives. It is highly unlikely that God actually told you to hit your sister.

Theology of Glory item	Why it's a Theology of Glory
Songs with lines like "Still the greatest treasure remains for those who gladly choose you now."	These songs glorify the one singing—and "choosing"—rather than the one to whom the song is being sung.
The claim from "religious" persons that you must somehow become less sinful and more saintly before God will accept you.	This suggests that it's up to you to become worthy to receive God's grace; this opposes the fact that while we were God's enemies, "we were reconciled to God through the death of his Son" (Romans 5:10).
The "religious" insistence that you must "decide" to accept Jesus as your Lord and Savior before he can save you.	If it's up to you to decide to be saved then you are not being saved by Jesus. Instead, you are saving yourself by virtue of your perceived ability to make the right decision.
Explanations for untimely deaths and other tragedies, like, "God took her because he needed another angel in heaven," or, "The Lord allowed his death in order to prevent greater suffering."	Theologians of glory typically believe they can get inside God's mind, forgetting the part where God says, "My thoughts are not your thoughts, nor are your ways my ways" (Isaiah 55:8).
The claim that the Bible contains a code about future events and that you can know exactly how these future events will play out.	The only thing certain about Christian "millennialism," as this view is known, is that for two millennia Christians have attempted to predict the future and for two millennia these predictions have been wrong.
Claims regarding who is going to heaven and who is going to that other place.	In the Apostles' Creed, Christians confess that Jesus will "come again to judge the living and the dead." Only a theologian of glory is presumptuous enough to take over a role that properly belongs to Christ.

What a Theologian of the Cross would say about it
Much better to sing about what Christ has done, is doing, and will do *for you*, rather than to boast about what you have done, are doing, or will do for Christ.
As Luther observed, "The Love of God does not find, but creates that which is pleasing to it."
"Free will after the fall exists in name only," Luther said. Human will is bound to choose against God and only God can free the mind and heart for faith.
"That person does not deserve to be called a theologian who looks upon the invisible things of God as though they were clearly perceptible in those things which have actually happened," Luther famously said. God acts most often "behind-the-scenes," doing work that we cannot know. The apostle Paul's confession: "O the depth of the riches and wisdom and knowledge of God! How unsearchable are God's judgments and how inscrutable God's ways!" (Romans 11:33). [Have fun and learn! Add your own!]

HOW TO TELL THE DIFFERENCE BETWEEN THE KINGDOM ON THE LEFT AND THE KINGDOM ON THE RIGHT

When Pilate asked Jesus whether he was the king of the Jews, he replied, "My kingdom is not of this world" (John 18:36). This statement has been the starting point of a long series of attempts to define the relationship between Christians and the world. Do Christians have a right to self-defense or civil disobedience? Can they sue their neighbors? Can they serve in the army when God commands us not to kill and Christ commands us to love the enemy? While there is no easy answer to many of these questions, Lutherans tend to favor a set of guiding principles rather than pat answers. Among these principles is Martin Luther's distinction between God's two kingdoms: the earthly or left-handed kingdom, and the heavenly or right-handed kingdom.

This distinction aims to do three things:

- To help Christians live as God's freed and forgiven people in a fallen and sinful world (you don't need to renounce the world and live in a monastery to be holy in God's eyes).
- To clarify that, although God is love and rules the church by love and forgiveness, God uses the force of the law to prevent people from destroying the world and hurting others. At the same time, God uses the law to drive people from one kingdom (on the left) into the other (on the right).

God's Kingdom on the Left. *God's Kingdom on the Right.*

The Lutheran interpretation of God's two kingdoms says they exist in exactly the same place and at exactly the same time, but that God governs differently in each.

- To guide the church in its relationships with the world, especially government, so that Christians understand their main mission to be preaching the gospel to other sinners, as well as their responsibility to speak out against unjust government whenever necessary.

These kingdoms exist in the exact same place, but operate in two distinct ways, or rather, God is the sovereign of the *whole* world and *governs* in two ways:

1. God governs all people in the earthly kingdom through the agency of secular government and the law (by means of force or conviction of sin).
2. Conversely, God rules all people who live by faith in Christ, or those in the spiritual kingdom, with God's right hand, through the gospel (by grace).

Discerning the two kingdoms is quite difficult sometimes and requires a light touch, but it gets easier with practice. Here are some steps to consider.

Kingdom on the Left	Kingdom on the Right
1. Note the restraint of evil. In the left-hand realm, laws and rules set limits against evildoers and God keeps people from being victimized.	Listen for the sound of mercy. You can trust God's promise of forgiveness of sins and obtain life and salvation.
2. Seek out institutions that provide safety and security, like families, governments, and the church. God gives structure to your life through them.	Spend time in places where God provides absolution, faithful preaching, and the sacraments of Baptism and Communion.
3. Look for the places where God provides opportunities for employment, creativity, and social harmony. That's where God is helping life flourish.	Look for sinners who confess that's what they are. You're bound to find them pointing to Jesus as the one who brought them into this realm.
4. Locate the times and places where sinners come to the end of their ropes. God uses the demands of this kingdom to push them into the other one.	When you find the kingdom on the right, you can be sure the promises God used to bring you there are true.

Be Aware

- Strictly speaking, neither the term "two kingdoms" nor "two reigns" is used in the Lutheran Confessions, yet both terms have become deeply embedded in Lutheran theology.
- Sinners regularly get the kingdoms confused and try to make each function like the other. Keeping the Ten Commandments and establishing a social order are important on the left, but they're not the same as the kingdom on the right. Any time we try to make our work on the left apply on the right, we deny Christ's work on the cross, which is the only thing that applies there.
- The kingdom on the left needs you to think about how you can participate to promote the well-being of creation. But human reason doesn't work so well in the other kingdom. All you can do there is simply trust that God's promise in the gospel will fully bring in God's will. Only the gospel can truly free people and reorient them to be genuinely concerned for others.

HOW TO TELL IF YOUR WILL IS IN BONDAGE TO SIN AND WHAT TO DO ABOUT IT

Lutherans are among the very few groups that openly, repeatedly, and almost embarrassingly confess that their will is NOT free with respect to sin and salvation and that they, in fact, will wrongly choose sin over faith in Jesus Christ, if given the opportunity. And it is precisely *because* the human will is bound to sin that Christ's death and resurrection are necessary. Still, we forget this from time to time and imagine our wills to be godlike and free.

People whose wills are in bondage to sin exhibit several symptoms. This exercise will help you identify those symptoms:

❶ Perform the following test:
Using the index and middle fingers of one hand, find your pulse (the wrist, neck, and under the arm are all good places to find your pulse). If a pulse is detected, your will is in bondage. (If no pulse is detected, dial 911. You've got bigger problems than a bound will.)

❷ Look for these symptoms:
- You feel a sense of helplessness and hopelessness after reading the Ten Commandments, like there's no way you can do it.
- You constantly want more or better stuff, such as clothes, money, electronics, and so on.
- You occasionally experience envy of persons who have more or better stuff than you.
- You find it easy to neglect the needs of others in favor of your own needs.

- You do (or desire to do) things you know in your mind you should not do.
- Even at your best you find it impossible to break the cycle and become "good."

❸ Reorient your thinking to what the Bible says about sin and human will.

Although many Christians speak of having a "free will," Lutherans believe that human will is bound to sin. As the apostle Paul writes, "For I do not do the good I want, but the evil I do not want is what I do" (Romans 7:19). The necessary remedy lies in Jesus Christ's death and resurrection. If you are not Jesus Christ, you need him.

Confessing in public that your will is bound to sin and that you cannot free yourself will help reorient you toward the One whose will is not bound to sin and who can, in fact, free you.

Once a bound will is identified:

❹ Admit it to yourself.
By admitting that you are in bondage to sin and cannot free yourself you become open to the promises, forgiveness, and surprises of God.

❺ Confess it in public.
This is slightly different than admitting it. It is one thing to tell yourself that you're sinful. It is another thing to say it out loud to someone else. Confession means admitting out loud, to someone else or in the company of other sinners, that you are in bondage to sin and in need of Christ.

❻ Listen actively for God's promises.
Your confession of sinfulness in worship, to a pastor, or to another Christian should always be followed by words of God's forgiveness. Be confident in God's promise of forgiveness.

❼ Move forward as the New Adam or New Eve that Christ has made you through your baptism.
Having admitted and confessed your bondage to sin, and having heard the promises of God, now is time to get over it and get on with living. Even though we are in bondage to sin, God simultaneously gives us the power to be children of God to live a godly life.

❽ Repeat daily.
Living in bondage to sin is not easy and requires constant confession and forgiveness.

HOW TO TELL THE DIFFERENCE BETWEEN A LUTHERAN PIETIST AND A LUTHERAN CONFESSIONALIST

While all claim the same theological ancestry, not all Lutherans are cut from the same cloth. Although often indistinguishable from one another physically, Pietists and Confessionalists represent two common and distinct "takes" on the Lutheran heritage. Your ability to discern the type of Lutheran in your company will help you navigate unfamiliar social terrain, participate in civil conversation, and craft an appropriate spontaneous table prayer should one become necessary.

❶ Evaluate the context and environment.
If you are at a Bible study, hymn sing, or prayer meeting, you are almost certainly among Pietists. If you are at poker night, a pub, or a barn dance, your host is likely a Confessionalist.

❷ Observe the person's facial expressions, especially around the eyes.
When speaking of Jesus, a Pietist will often become misty and unfocused. If your companion's gaze is disconcertingly clear and piercing, however, she or he is a Confessionalist.

Note the closed eyes and warm heart of the Lutheran Pietist as she sings her favorite hymn from memory.

Some Lutheran Confessionalists find reading the creeds a helpful distraction from theologically substandard preaching.

❸ Discreetly note whether the person is carrying published material and what it is.
While either type of Lutheran may carry a Bible, supplementary material will differ. Look for Philip Jacob Spener's *Pia Desideria* (Pious Desires) in the hands of a Pietist. Confessionalist Lutherans may have the weightier *Book of Concord* tucked under an arm or in a satchel.

❹ Examine patterns of wear on the person's personal copy of the Bible.
To the trained eye, the stains that edge the pages of a person's Bible are like blinking neon signs. The Pietist's Bible will be especially well-thumbed at the "spiritual" Gospel of John. Look for extensive wear along the pages of Paul's letter to the Romans in the Confessionalist's Bible.

5 Listen for telltale jargon.
Headier by nature, Confessionalists will want to talk theology, and may use the phrase "justified by grace through faith" to settle almost any question. More concerned with matters of the heart, a Pietist may want to talk about your mutual love of Jesus.

6 Note what they do with the hymnal.
A Pietist will know the hymns by heart and sing them from memory, often with eyes closed. A hymnal may be held against the chest with one or both hands. Confessional Lutherans prefer to read the hymns rather than sing them, and have been known to use such hymnal reading as a means of self-defense against evangelically inadequate preaching.

7 Rely on instinct when the above steps fail.
Generally speaking, if you feel like a sinner, you're with Pietists. If you feel pretty normal but have been called a sinner one or more times, you're with Confessionalists.

Be Aware

- Most Lutheran churches contain both Pietists and Confessionalists, although ratios will vary. Both types take their faith seriously and love the Bible, Jesus, and their neighbors. Neither is widely regarded as "better" or "smarter" or "more faithful."
- Differences in the language used to talk about faith and differences in personal pieties may lead to misunderstandings that are best worked out through conversation, generosity, and fellowship. Avoid starting a fight.

HOW TO TELL THE DIFFERENCE BETWEEN ORIGINAL SIN AND EVERYDAY SIN

Probably due to the lack of clarity they experience in popular culture and the relative unpleasantness of the subject matter, many Lutherans occasionally commit the minor heresy of confusing *original sin* and *everyday sins*. As with most complex theological issues, the Lutheran method of bringing understanding is to stop and draw a careful distinction.

❶ Clarify your terms.
- Original sin is what many theologians call "the unavoidable desire of humans to disobey God." Original sin is not something that we do; it is something that causes us to do things. It helps to think about original sin as *human sinfulness*.
- Everyday sins are the faithless and stupid things humans do because we are still in the grip of original sin. Everyday sins include things like lying or cheating to get ahead, and intentionally hurting or misusing our bodies or the bodies of others. Everyday sins are sinful *acts*, the kinds of things forbidden in the Ten Commandments.

❷ Revisit the basic relationship between cause and effect.
Original sin is the *reason* that we are tempted to commit everyday sins. In the strange calculus of sin, original sin is the cause; everyday sins are the effects. Put another way, original sin relates to who we *are*; everyday sins relate to what we *do*.

❸ Sharpen the distinction to its finest point.
Original sin and everyday sins are not two different
kinds of the same thing. In yet another metaphor,
everyday sins are symptoms of the underlying sickness of
original sin.

❹ Listen carefully to the language around the terms;
take them in context.
If the word *sin* is being used in a way that makes it seem
completely *unavoidable*, it is probably being used to mean
original sin. For example. "Because of *sin* in the world,
there will always be war." On the other hand, if the
word *sin* is being used in a way that makes it seem like
something you could avoid doing, it is probably being
used to mean everyday sin For example: "I am tempted
to sin by disobeying my mother."

Be Aware

- Saying original sin is a cause of your sin, as though
  "the devil made me do it," does NOT get you off the
  hook. It's still *your* sin.
- Confusing original sin and everyday sin does not, in
  itself, qualify as a sin. It's just imperfect judgment.
- While sinfulness and sins are realities in the Christian
  life, Lutherans know that they are only the last gasps of
  an enemy that Jesus has defeated forever. Jesus forgives
  our everyday sins and has freed us finally from the grip
  of original sin. We are freed and called to be the faithful
  servants of God we were created to be!

HOW TO TELL THE DIFFERENCE BETWEEN A SINNER AND A SAINT

Many Christians claim they can tell the difference between saints and sinners. Sinners are naughty and do naughty things, they say, and saints are nice and do nice things. For Lutherans, however, who strive to take an honest and searching inventory of human nature, distinguishing saint from sinner has never been easy.

❶ **Grapple briefly with the following question: "Can the finite bear the infinite?"**
Originally used by the church to help resolve the debate over whether Jesus was all man (completely human) *or* all God (completely divine), this question can be useful when discerning sinner from saint. Lutherans answer the question by saying, "Yes!" Baptism makes the finite (you) able to bear the infinite (Christ), so it's not a matter of naughty *or* nice, sinner *or* saint (or, in Jesus' case, man *or* God). A person is fully a saint and fully a sinner at the same time.

❷ **Embrace the sinner so that the saint can be revealed. Avoid pulling punches.**
Fearlessly and truthfully answer the question, "Am I (or, are you) a sinner?" based strictly on the evidence at hand. (Hint: when in doubt simply measure yourself or the other person against the Ten Commandments.) If you hedge by saying, "No, not totally. I keep some commandments sometimes," you are blissfully deluded.

❸ **Bone up on what the Bible says about it.**
Scripture makes clear that being a sinner is a prerequisite for being a saint (see Romans 5:8; Galatians 2:17; and Matthew 9:13). Why else would a saint like the apostle Paul "boast" that he was himself the chief of sinners (1 Timothy 1:15)? Why else would he confess that "I do not do the good I want but the evil I do not want is what I do"?

❹ **Employ standard, Lutheran "two-handed" thinking.**
On the one hand, people are sinners when they disobey God's Commandments and when they doubt or disbelieve the Word of God. The end of such sinners is death. On the other hand, people are saints when they are justified by faith in Christ apart from the works of the law and when they continue to trust and believe God's promises in Christ. The end of such saints is eternal life.

Be Aware

- Although Christians are exhorted to "tame the flesh," they can't make themselves "less of a sinner" over time. You can't become, say, 35 percent sinner and 65 percent saint if you just work really hard at it. You can't change the percentages of sinner/saint within you.
- Traditionally, Lutherans have preferred to use the Latin phrase *simul iustus et peccator*, where *iustus* = "justified one" or "saint" and *peccator* = "sinner." (See "Seven Complicated Lutheran Theological Terms in Latin and What They Mean in Plain English" on page 161.)

HOW TO TELL THE DIFFERENCE BETWEEN A LUTHERAN CONSERVATIVE AND A LUTHERAN LIBERAL

All movements, whether religious, political, social, or economic, contain a spectrum of belief that ranges from the far right (conservative) to the far left (liberal) within their own contexts. The Lutheran movement is no different, gladly embracing widely divergent perspectives under a single banner. Knowing the far right from the far left can assist the outside observer in gaining the much needed perspective to keep from laughing at people at parties when they act all weird and extremist.

While certain characteristics are common to both ends of the spectrum, under close examination key differences reveal themselves.

1 Note a tendency toward absolutes; extremists rely upon them heavily.
In the case of conservatives, this manifests in the form of universal pronouncements in the strong, literal verbiage of 16th-century Saxony regarding Truth and Eternity. Liberals prefer the language of an imaginary "correctness" etiquette, whose claims to truth are equally strong but slightly more implied.

2 Listen for the consistent use of superlatives.
Extremists of both stripes commonly use the words *always* and *never* in theological conversations, such as, "Luther *never* said that," "Melanchthon *always* did," or "One must *always* speak of God's love but *never* God's judgment."

❸ Take careful notice of the subject's bookshelves. Conservative Lutherans are likely to own—and have read—the entire 55 volumes of *Luther's Works* (truly hardcore conservatives may own all 117 quarto volumes of Weimar Edition, published in the original Latin and German), a Bible, a dog-eared copy of *The Lutheran Confessions*, and little else. Liberals probably own volume 53 on "Liturgy and Hymns," a copy of the Confessions, the complete works of Dietrich Bonhoeffer, an anthology of poetry, and subscribe to several social justice periodicals.

The Lutheran movement embraces widely divergent points of view. Can you tell which is the conservative and which is the liberal?

④ Examine the physical features for specific types of wear and fatigue.

A conservative's eyes, for example, tend to be narrow with significant wrinkling around the edges due to rigorous peering at the fine print of footnotes, glossaries, and indexes. Typical to a liberal's physicality are softer hands, wider eyes, and a more "correct" posture when seated. Conservatives tend toward mustaches and tight-necked apparel while liberals often have beards and wear looser, free-flowing clothing. (This refers to both genders in each case.)

⑤ Discern carefully the two distinct modes of activism.

Conservative Lutherans perceive an assault on the purity of Lutheran doctrine from the left and often produce small, independent, underground publications decorated with Luther's Seal and peppered with strongly worded citations from the Confessions against ecumenism. Liberals perceive an assault on the openness and diversity of Lutheranism from the right, and usually make placards, wear sandals, and march in favor of ecumenism.

Be Aware

- Ecumenism is not the only issue that divides conservative and liberal Lutherans. There are a few others.
- Most theologians and historians hold that the Lutheran movement's ability to accommodate a wide spectrum of belief while continuing to hold its center is a characteristic of its strength and durability.
- Some Lutherans disagree with the "holding its center" part.

THE FOUR MOST COMMON HERESIES WELL-INTENTIONED LUTHERANS COMMIT

Heresy means a belief or opinion contrary to orthodox religious doctrine. While in Luther's time heresy often arose from well-intentioned reform, rebellion, or misguided ambition, nowadays people typically hold such beliefs due to misunderstanding or out of a simple lack of information, not direct opposition. Still, even "good" Lutherans need a primer on heresy from time to time.

❶ We are saved by grace through faith in Jesus Christ, *plus* our good works.
Lutherans confess that we are made right with God by God's grace through faith in Jesus, and not by what we do. But many Lutherans continue to believe, deep down, that the good you do somehow, in some way, helps "get you into heaven"—and, conversely, that your sins can cause God to "unsave" you. This is categorically false. Salvation comes undeserved only through the gift of faith in Christ.

❷ Theology of glory with a veneer of theology of the cross.
Lutherans believe that Jesus' death on the cross is the surprising way God chose to rescue people from sin and death. The cross reveals a God who is present in suffering and uses what is weak or broken to fulfill God's promises. Instead of this theology of the cross, some Lutherans adopt a theology of glory, with a God who promises health, wealth, and happiness to all who believe "hard enough."

Marcionism.

Marcion, a notorious heretic, dismissed the Old Testament God as mean and judgmental—a God only of the law. Marcion insisted that God was all love and cut the Old Testament out of his Bible. While Lutherans tend to prefer love to judgment, and gospel to law, without the law to reveal our sin and serious need for God, even a loving God is unnecessary. *Note:* Like Marcion, well-intentioned Lutherans also are sometimes guilty of picking and choosing what scriptures they will accept as authoritative, which is not the same thing as Luther's understanding of the "canon within the canon." (See page 252.)

Not-so-real presence.

Lutheran doctrine speaks of Jesus' "real presence" in Holy Communion. That means Jesus' body and blood are truly present "in, with, and under" the bread and wine that are "given and shed for you." We simply take Jesus at his word when he says, "This *is* my body." Some Lutherans, however, mistake this real presence for a symbolic presence, a memorial representation of the Last Supper intended *only* as a remembrance. This is regrettable, since it cuts them off from a promised point of contact with Christ.

Be Aware

- Capital punishment is no longer a threat against heresy in most places, as it was in Luther's time when the church often burned heretics at the stake—even though some people still wish it were today.

HOW TO SHOW THE WORLD YOU'RE A LUTHERAN WITHOUT BEING FLASHY OR BORING

There are dozens of Christian traditions in North America, each emphasizing a slightly different aspect of the Christian faith, and many more people of other faiths. While Lutherans tend toward humility and prefer to avoid the spotlight, we should not be shy about sharing our Christian faith or our Lutheran way of understanding and living that faith.

Showing the world you're a Lutheran can be accomplished in part by means of a bumper sticker, but this should not represent the totality of your faith expression.

❶ Strive always to see the divine in things the world considers to be mundane, boring, or weak.
Lutherans are famous for finding pearls hidden among swine and strength hidden in weakness. Adopting this philosophy equips you with the ability to dethrone worldly powers and proclaim Christ.

❷ Confess your faith status in plain language, unostentatiously and without fanfare.
When talking with someone about faith or religion, simply say, "I am Lutheran," or "I am a Lutheran Christian." (You should be ready to explain what being Lutheran means to you, in case someone asks.)

❸ Consider adorning yourself, your home, or your vehicle with simple Lutheran accoutrements. Avoid garish colors and bold fonts where possible.
Wear a Luther's Rose pendant or display the Luther's Rose at your home in the form of a cross-stitched mural, in your office in the form of a paperweight or on your e-mail signature, or on your car in the form of a bumper sticker.

❹ Adopt a policy of celebrating life events with a note of service to the neighbor.
For a friend or family member's next birthday, make a gift to a Lutheran social service agency (such as Lutheran Disaster Relief or Lutheran Immigration and Refugee Service) in that person's honor. *Note:* Some non-Lutherans may not "get" the value of this kind of celebration; consider also giving that person a gift card to their favorite fast-food restaurant to avoid hurt feelings.

Be Aware

- Martin Luther wrote that what makes a Christian shoemaker Christian is *not* that he puts crosses on his shoes, but that he makes good shoes. In this way, Luther cautions us that being Christian is not about the signs, symbols, or even the words we use, but about the way we live our lives.
- Many Lutherans live in ways that other Lutherans would call flashy, and vice versa. It's really a matter of perspective.
- Most non-Lutherans automatically associate the word *Lutheran* with the word *boring*. If you err to one side or the other, be flashier rather than more boring.

Martin Luther wrote that what makes a Christian shoemaker Christian is not that he puts crosses on his shoes, but that he makes good shoes. Being Christian is less about the symbols we use to adorn our lives, but the way we live our lives.

HOW TO HANDLE YOURSELF WHEN YOU GET ANGRY AT GOD

While anger may appear to run counter to worshiping God, irritation and even outright anger have been and continue to be legitimate emotions emanating from believers. Appropriate anger may be seen as part of the faithful believer's repertoire of sentiments when used sparingly and within reason.

❶ Identify the issues.
Directing anger at God serves as a natural response in certain situations, including the sudden death of a loved one or unanswered prayers. However, the source of anger may not always be clear. In such situations, take time, perhaps silently, to identify the basis of your anger.

❷ Evaluate your response.
Consider whether your level of hostility compares to what you perceive God's transgression to be. Not getting a raise or failing a test may provoke a generalized sense of anger that includes the Almighty, but nonetheless should be directed elsewhere.

❸ Watch your mouth.
Anger is acceptable; disrespect is not. Keep the Commandments at all times. Avoid dishonoring or slandering God.

❹ Avoid physical violence.
Reject taking out anger on other people, places, or things. Wrestling with God has been attempted, but seldom proves fruitful and can lead to hip dislocation and a residual limp. (See Genesis 32:24.)

❺ Consider taking a time-out.
Shunning worship is not advised. Use communion time for prayer and continued dialogue with God.

❻ Review the history of humans getting angry with God.
You're not the first person to get angry with God, and you won't be the last. Read Scripture to identify how others have worked through "righteous" fury. Note occasional risk of smiting.

❼ Identify and accept your own responsibility.
Understanding what has caused your anger may lead to introspection and subsequent reassignment of responsibility.

❽ Make nice.
At the appropriate time, thank God for steadfastness through times of anger, for forgiving your outburst, and call it a truce.

Be Aware

- From time to time, anger at God may become non-descript and lingering. Recruiting the counsel of a third party may be wise when anger turns to bitterness. Conversations with a pastor or professional therapist may be valuable. For clergy, such counseling for anger toward God may fall under employee assistant programs under "work-related stress." Check your health-care benefit plan.

HOW TO INVITE A FRIEND OR NEIGHBOR TO CHURCH WITHOUT TERRIFYING THEM

Introverted and unostentatious by nature, Lutherans are often reserved in expressing their personal faith to others. Many fear that extending invitations to attend church may permanently scare off friends and neighbors or get them labeled as "Jesus freaks." Employing a natural and comfortable approach when inviting others, however, can ease this fear for everyone.

Sunday School Christmas program

newcomers to church

Regular church worship services can be too intimidating for some newcomers. Consider inviting them instead to a special event so they can "warm up" to the idea of church.

❶ Work consistently to develop open relationships with friends and neighbors.
While this may seem obvious, when it comes to an evangelistic lifestyle, an invitation to church is less likely to frighten those who know you well. An invitation to church may also be a way to deepen a relationship with a new acquaintance, too.

❷ Find a comfortable, personal language when you talk about your church; share experiences; avoid using clichés you've learned from popular culture.
Talk about people and events at your church as though they were a natural part of your life; and wouldn't it be nice if they actually were? If you had an uplifting experience during a worship service, share it. This may intrigue your friends and encourage them to ask questions.

❸ Make it a practice to talk frequently about your faith. Use "I" statements.
Share with your friends and neighbors why active participation in a community of faith is important to you. Talk about sermons that you find thought provoking and Bible studies where you learned something new. Putting these anecdotes in terms of your own experience can help avoid making others feel foisted upon.

❹ Consider doing a little foisting once in a while.
On rare occasions, the best move is gently to connect friends with your church through kindly force or coercion. For example, "kidnap" your friend on a Sunday morning and take him or her to church when your original invitation was "just for coffee." Or "just drop by" the church picnic on your way to the ballgame.

❺ Make simple, everyday connections between faith and daily living.
Explain the relationship you see between your faith and your daily living. How does attending church prepare you for the week ahead (or liberate you from the week behind)? Ask if they would like to share this experience.

❻ Use special events as unique opportunities.
"Regular church" can be too intimidating for some. Consider inviting friends and neighbors to a congregational special musical event such as the Christmas pageant, for example. Invite them to special dinners. Eating is both a necessary and nonthreatening activity. Ask them to join you on a mission trip or to help at the food bank.

❼ Encourage the children in your life to invite friends.
Young children and youth are often less threatening than adults and can be used quite shamelessly in service to the gospel. Encourage your children to invite their friends to church programs and worship services. Make it a condition of Saturday-night sleepovers that the whole household attends church the next day. This can lead to families attending together.

Be Aware

- Teaching yourself to accentuate the positive about your church will almost certainly have salutary effects on your evangelistic lifestyle.
- Complaining about people at your church is a poor reflection of both you and your church, and it will ultimately create greater terror in those whom you would invite.
- Words such as *witness, proselytize, testimony,* and *evangelism* can cause shaky knees and faint hearts among many un-churched, de-churched, or semi-churched persons. Use extreme caution when employing them in invitations.

HOW TO MEMORIZE LUTHER'S SMALL CATECHISM

Most people don't often think about the studs within the walls of their homes or the framework in the ceiling, but if these structures are not in place and true the whole house will come crashing down. For Lutherans, Martin Luther's Small Catechism serves a similar purpose; Christ is our true foundation and the Catechism provides a solid, user-friendly, time-tested framework for the household built on this foundation.

Even Luther said: "I study it daily and remain a pupil of the Catechism ... and I am convinced by experience that God's Word can never be entirely mastered" (*Luther's Works* 14:8). Here are a few tips to make sure your framework is in place and sturdy.

1 **Make a daily investment of time with the Catechism.**
The Small Catechism cannot do its work in the dusty past or buried in a desk drawer. Spend a few minutes each day reciting a section of it out loud. Schedule a routine time and stick to it. Also keep copies at your bedside, on your table, and on your toilet tank so you can read it on a regular basis.

Note to the technologically adept: Consider recording yourself reading the Catechism aloud as a digital sound file and transferring it to your mp3 player to further facilitate your daily reading/hearing.

There are many things Lutherans do every day.
A few minutes each day with the Small Catechism
can facilitate memorization and deepen your
faith journey at the same time.

❷ Segment your readings into digestible bits; avoid
doing too much at once.

Even though it is "small," cramming in the whole
Catechism is not advisable. Learn a section by heart,
then go on to another. For example, start with the Ten
Commandments themselves (just a few at a time) and
then go back and learn their meanings.

❸ Keep a sense of humor about the work of memorization.
Avoid allowing the Catechism to become a burdensome law to you. A long-term relationship with it is your primary goal, so keep things light as you go and stay consistent. (This is especially true for those who have children. At any age, kids need to get silly and playful. They may want to race through the words or sing them or pronounce them with a funny accent. THIS IS GOOD.)

❹ Find a verbatim musical version of the Catechism and learn to sing it.
Music is probably the most effective mnemonic device for memorization. A simple Internet search will reveal multiple options for purchase, some of which can easily be transferred to a computer or mp3 player.

❺ Explore the possibility of a regular Small Catechism/worship connection.
If your congregation doesn't already use the Small Catechism in worship in some way, talk to the worship committee or your pastor about giving it a try. For example: the explanation of one of the articles of the creed makes a great confession of faith. Deeply rooted Lutheran congregations often make booklet copies freely available to members and visitors alike.

❻ Endeavor to maintain a lifelong relationship with the Small Catechism.
As Luther says, we are never finished learning from the Catechism. To keep the framework of your internal faith structure sturdy and true, recite it aloud your whole life. Another way to do this is to pray the Catechism (a prayer version is available too).

Be Aware

- While many Lutherans maintain other daily disciplines, such as tooth brushing and gargling, they eschew daily routines around faith practices. The Small Catechism can become a foundational bulwark against faith decay and should not be underestimated as a personal resource.
- Parents are the primary teachers for their children and should avoid neglecting their calling. The best place for faith learning to happen is in the home, at the dinner table or bedside, wherever daily life and relationships are processed. The Small Catechism provides an exceptional framework for those conversations against which decisions and behavior can be measured and adjusted.

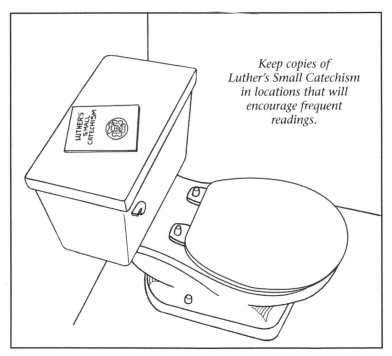

Keep copies of Luther's Small Catechism in locations that will encourage frequent readings.

BIBLE STUFF

A BRIEF HISTORY OF THE BIBLE

A smaller number in B.C. ("before Christ") time actually denotes a year that is later in history than the larger number. For example, events in 1500 B.C. happened after events that occurred in 1700 B.C. With A.D. *(Anno Domini,* or "The Year of Our Lord") dates, on the other hand, the years get progressively larger. The dates below are approximates.

Creation.
> God created the universe and everything in it; the things God created continue to create and procreate.

1700–1500 B.C. The Ancestors.
> God blesses Abraham and Sarah and their descendants so that they will in turn bless the rest of the world.

1240 B.C. The Exodus.
> God hears the groans of the people in Egypt and frees them from Pharaoh's slavery.

1240–1200 B.C. Sinai and Wilderness.
> God makes a covenant with the people at Mount Sinai and gives them laws, such as the Ten Commandments.

1200 B.C. The Land.
> God gives the people a land to live in.

1200–1000 B.C. Period of the Judges.
> God serves as the "King" of the twelve tribes of Israel so that they don't have to live under a human king. Leaders, known as "judges," serve as the human leaders under God's rule.

1000 B.C. The United Monarchy.
> The people want to be like other nations, so they demand a human king. Saul becomes Israel's first human king.

960 B.C. David.

God promises David that one of his descendants will forever be king of Israel; David moves the capital to Jerusalem.

940 B.C. Temple.

Solomon builds God a temple in Jerusalem.

922 B.C. The Divided Monarchy.

The nation splits in half because of bad leadership. The northern kingdom is called "Israel" and the southern kingdom is called "Judah."

922–722 B.C. Northern Kingdom.

Israel lasts until Assyria destroys it in 722 B.C. Its capital is Samaria; its descendants are called Samaritans.

922–587 B.C. Southern Kingdom.

Judah lasts until Babylon destroys Jerusalem and its temple in 587 B.C. Its descendants are called Jews. During these years, first editions of many books of the Old Testament are written.

587–539 B.C. Exile and Diaspora.*

The leaders of the people live in Babylon in exile until Babylon is conquered and they can return home. Many of them never return home, so God's people spread out across the world.

520–450 B.C. Rebuilding Judea.

Some exiled people return and rebuild the temple and Jerusalem. The people are not their own nation, but a province of Persia. Many books of the Old Testament reach their final form during these years.

---

* "Diaspora" refers to the populations of Jews exiled from Judea in this time, who were disbursed to surrounding and neighboring lands.

330 B.C. **Greek Rule.**
   The Greeks conquer the Holy Land and rule Judea.

67 B.C. **Roman Rule.**
   The Romans conquer the Holy Land and rule Judea.
   By this time, all of the books of the Old Testament are
   completed.

4 B.C. **The Christ.**
   Jesus Christ is born.

A.D. 26–29. **Jesus' Public Ministry.**
   Jesus ministers, teaches, and preaches publicly. He calls
   his first followers.

A.D. 29. **Crucifixion and Resurrection**
   Jesus is crucified and raised from the dead.

A.D. 29. **Pentecost.**
   God sends the Holy Spirit and the church is born.

A.D. 35. **Paul's Conversion.**
   Saul, a persecutor of the church, converts and becomes a
   leading evangelist.

A.D. 50–100. **New Testament Written.**
   The documents that later became part of the New
   Testament are written.

In 67 B.C. the Romans conquered the Holy Land, but the Old Testament books had pretty much been completed by then anyway.

HOW TO CHOOSE A BIBLE TRANSLATION THAT'S RIGHT FOR YOU

Unless you already read biblical Hebrew, Aramaic, and Greek, you need a Bible translation. You could go learn these languages, but someone's already done the work for you. Choose wisely to enjoy a lifetime relationship with the Scriptures.

❶ Examine yourself and your motivations.
Think about who you are and why you want to explore the Bible. Do you need a simple Bible or a more nuanced translation? Is this Bible for devotional use or for in-depth study? Do you need one with lots of pictures and small words?

❷ Consider a Bible printed in a language you actually speak.
For example, if thou dost not maketh use of words like *dost* or *maketh*, picketh thou another translation.

❸ Seek an actual translation, not a paraphrased version.
A paraphrase is a rewording of the Bible, an interpretation of a translation. This is like making a photocopy of a photocopy; resolution and clarity start to diminish. Look on the title page or preface for a phrase like "translated from the original languages."

❹ **Determine the translation's level of faithfulness to the original wording.**
Look for footnotes offering alternative translations or that point out where the biblical texts are difficult and the meaning uncertain. Translators often make tough choices; good translations clue you in.

❺ **Read a familiar passage.**
Can you understand what you are reading? Does it help you hear God's word anew? Consider a passage *other* than John 3:16.

Unless you can read biblical Hebrew, Aramaic, and Greek, you might want to find yourself a good translation in a language you understand.

❻ Clarify your need for "helps."
Does the translation include introductions and explanations by reputable scholars? Such comments are not a part of the Bible, but can be a real plus in understanding the text, especially for serious study. Some study Bibles use call-outs and discussion questions to add another interesting dimension to Scripture reading.

Be Aware

- Jesus speaks to us through the Bible. Reading an accurate, understandable translation can result in radical life transformations, spiritual maturity, and actual growth in faith.
- Unless you actually carry your Bible around with you everywhere, do not purchase a nylon cover with zipper and pockets. They're geeky.

HOW TO READ THE ENTIRE BIBLE IN ONE YEAR

Reading the entire Bible is a formidable task and can frustrate even the most patient believer when approached willy-nilly. A measured and consistent walk through the Bible, however, can be done without tremendous fuss. Also, when you're finished you can boast that you've read the entire Bible.

❶ **Consider purchasing a good "one-year" Bible.** Many good translations are published also in one-year editions. This tool can make the job much easier. It should combine daily Old and New Testament readings with a psalm or section from Proverbs.

❷ **Choose a method that matches your personality and reading habits.**
- Start with one book and skip around. Begin with one of the four Gospels, such as John, then read an Old Testament book, like Genesis. Jump to one of the epistles, such as Ephesians. Skipping around keeps your attention fresh.
- Start with the first page and read straight through to the last. This is a common method for Lutherans, who are typically organized in their Bible reading. Keep in mind the first 10 books of the Bible can get fact-heavy and dry. Plowing through them may wear you out fast. If this occurs, try skipping to the juicy parts for variety.

When attempting to read the entire Bible in one year, avoid reading late at night, as this will promote an unwelcome association between God's word and drowsiness.

❸ Covenant with a reading buddy or accountability group.
Commit to each other that you will do your daily readings aloud together when possible and that you'll keep up with them when it's not. Agree to penalties for skipped days.

❹ Celebrate your completed reading of the Bible.
At the end of your Year of the Bible, consider holding a ritual in which you thank God for the experience.

Be Aware

- You do not earn your salvation by reading the Bible, but you will experience growth in faith. Allow the Scriptures to speak to you.
- Many good translations include a suggested one-year reading schedule broken into daily chunks.
- A good bookmark can be almost as important to daily reading as the reading itself. Find one you look forward to seeing each day when you open the book.
- Avoid trying to read as much as you can each sitting. Set limits for yourself or you won't keep your patriarchs straight.
- Avoid reading late at night. Dozing off in the middle of the history books guarantees a later reread.

HOW TO START A BIBLE STUDY GROUP

Bible studies can be a source of great insight and growth, or they can become a regular chore populated with people you don't like too much. Starting your own group can be a good way to invite the former rather than the latter. Support the entire process with prayer.

1 Consider the composition of your group and make personal invitations.
You may want to study with a diverse group, with people like you, or with folks unlike you. Pray for discernment. A respectful, face-to-face invitation is typically most effective. Allow invitees time to consider their response, and give assurances that a "no" answer carries no threat of Lutheran guilt.

2 Pick a comfortable, neutral location.
Consider doing this together during your first gathering. A coffee shop sets a different tone from a Sunday school classroom. Find a location that meets your needs and pray that it serves your study. Keep in mind people's need for good lighting, coffee, and access to restrooms.

3 Choose a regular, recurring meeting time as a group.
While you cannot meet everyone's schedule, you can guarantee that you won't get young people on Friday night or business people during the workday.

❹ Consider pursuing a theme or collective subject of interest.
Whether you work with a curriculum or let the group self-govern, having some kind of cohesive concept keeps up interest. Pray together for guidance.

❺ Maintain a humble attitude about your role.
Study leadership can be shared. Welcome guest speakers or rotate the job of leader around the group. Pray for wisdom.

When convening your Bible study group for the first time, be sure to choose a location that will be neutral and comfortable for all participants, not just yourself.

❻ Stay consistent.

Try not to change the time or location, and keep talking about it to others. Pray for God to remain present and active.

Be Aware

- Fully inform people at the time of invitation regarding the commitment they'd be making by joining your group.
- Many groups like the "round robin" approach to using each other's homes as study group locations—for the variety, and a chance to examine one another's bathrooms and medicine cabinets.
- Becoming dogmatic or authoritarian about meeting times and attendance is a big turn-off and is counter-productive. Give folks a break once in a while.

THE FIVE GROSSEST BIBLE DISEASES

❶ The Plague (1 Samuel 5–6).
This plague was most likely an outbreak of bubonic plague. Translations say the people were struck with "tumors," swelling caused by mice-borne infection, which resulted in death.

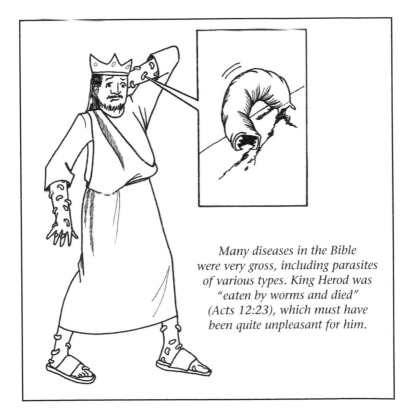

Many diseases in the Bible were very gross, including parasites of various types. King Herod was "eaten by worms and died" (Acts 12:23), which must have been quite unpleasant for him.

❷ Parasites (Acts 12:23).
According to this account, Herod was "eaten by worms and died." Abdominal parasites may be acquired when one eats contaminated food. The infected food fights back and eats one's intestinal organs.

❸ Leprosy (see Leviticus 14, etc.).
The biblical disease described in English translations as "leprosy" is not modern leprosy (Hansen's disease), which results in the deterioration of nerves and bodily extremities. Biblical lepers suffered from fungal infections of the skin and had chronic scaly and patchy skin. This was often accompanied by a repugnant odor.

❹ Discharges (Leviticus 15:2; Numbers 5:2, etc.).
Many biblical diseases resulted in painful and unpleasant discharges from various parts of the body. These diseases likely included gonorrhea and other infectious diseases.

❺ Boils and Blains (Exodus 9:10).
A boil is essentially an inflamed, pus-filled swelling on the skin, typically caused by the infection of a hair follicle. A very popular biblical disease, it is often the result of poor personal hygiene, bad luck, or God's wrath, depending. A blain is like a boil but may not involve the hair follicle.

TOP FIVE SCARY MONSTERS IN THE BIBLE

① **The Red Dragon (Revelation 12).**
This serpentine creature has seven heads with a crown on each, plus 10 horns. This dragon not only opposes God but also ultimately reveals itself as the devil.

Monsters in the Bible are often described as quite scary. The red dragon in Revelation 12 is one of the scarier ones. Lutherans tend to look somewhat askance at monsters.

❷ The Beast from the Sea (Revelation 13).
Not to be confused with the red dragon or Leviathan, this otherworldly fiend gains all his power from the dragon and makes others swear allegiance to him. He bears the unlikely combination of a leopard's body, a bear's feet, and a lion's mouth. His seven heads each bear blasphemous names, along with 10 horns and 10 crowns.

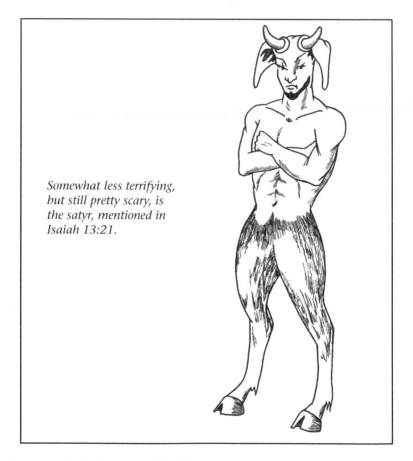

Somewhat less terrifying, but still pretty scary, is the satyr, mentioned in Isaiah 13:21.

❸ Rahab (Isaiah 51).
A mythical sea monster from Babylonian legend, she represents chaos and destruction—not to mention the pagan faith opposing the Israelites. (The Rahab from Isaiah 51 should not be confused with the woman mentioned in Joshua 2:1-21; 6:17-25; and Matthew 1:5.)

❹ Leviathan (Job 3).
Since the sea represented the chaotic unknown to the Israelites, anything living in it scared them. Even though Leviathan was likely just a whale, the very fact that it lived in the abyss made it creepy.

❺ Satyrs or Goat-Demons (Isaiah 13:21).
A satyr, also popular in Greek mythology, is a man with goat legs, ears, and horns. Popular images of Satan are often derived from this creature.

TOP SEVEN DASTARDLY BIBLE DEEDS

The Bible is adult literature. It is about real life and does not sugarcoat it. The Bible includes countless tales of murder, theft, sexual assault, and of people breaking every commandment in graphic detail.

❶ Adam and Eve sin (Genesis 3).
Eve and Adam ate the forbidden fruit: the first sin. Adam blamed it on his wife. The earth was cursed because of their sin.

Perhaps the most dastardly deed in the Bible is Adam and Eve's original sin, the one that started it all.

❷ Cain kills Abel (Genesis 4).
Brothers Cain and Abel both offered God gifts. Cain offered God's gifts from the cursed earth, so God liked Abel's gift better. In a jealous fit, Cain killed Abel, but God had mercy on Cain and did not kill him in return.

❸ Pharoah's tyranny (Exodus 1–15).
Pharaoh grew afraid of the Israelites in his country, so he enslaved them. When they grew too numerous, he ordered that all newborn boys be killed. Even after he agreed to let the people go, Pharaoh changed his mind and pursued the people with his army.

❹ David takes Bathsheba, kills Uriah (2 Samuel 11).
King David's personal life included more dastardly deeds than any television miniseries ever dreamed up. David had sex with Bathsheba, Uriah's wife, and then sent Uriah to a certain death in battle to cover it up.

❺ Herod slaughters the innocents (Matthew 2:1-18).
When the Wise Men told King Herod that they had come to worship the child who had been born as the new King of the Jews, Herod tried to trick the Wise Men into leading him to the child. When that failed, he ordered that all boys under two years of age be killed.

❻ Jesus' crucifixion (Mark 14–15).
Crucifixion was an exceptionally dastardly way of torturing a person to death. The victim did not bleed to death, but slowly died from asphyxiation due to the weight of his or her own body. The Roman governor Pilate and other authorities knew Jesus was innocent, but allowed the people to crucify him anyway.

Saul persecutes the church (Acts 1–9).
Saul of Tarsus persecuted the church, trying to stomp out those who followed Jesus. But as Paul, he repented and became a follower of Jesus himself. God's mercy is wide enough to forgive any dastardly deed.

TOP SEVEN ACTS OF HUMAN KINDNESS IN THE BIBLE

For all its shocking violence, the acts of mercy and kindness described in the Bible are perhaps even more shocking. The scandalous thing is that the people who offer kindness are often the people we would least expect to do so.

❶ Esau, the better brother? (Genesis 32).
Jacob stole Esau's birthright. Decades later, Esau goes to meet Jacob with 400 armed men. Remembering Esau's vow to kill him, Jacob is terrified. But Esau runs to meet him with heartfelt tears and generous gifts.

❷ Joseph pities his brothers (Genesis 50).
Joseph's brothers threw him in a pit and sold him into slavery. Years later, when he could make them pay, he repays them with gifts and the offer of a new life with him in Egypt.

❸ Pharaoh's daughter pulls Moses from the reeds (Exodus 2).
Pharaoh's daughter saves Moses from a soggy death and adopts him as her own son. The pagan princess holds the power of life and changes everything for God's people.

❹ Naomi adopts Ruth (Ruth 1).
After the death of both of their husbands, daughter-in-law Ruth chooses to remain with Naomi and share her life and faith, rather than return to her own home. Here devotion, hope, and love become one.

Acts of kindness in the Bible are usually committed by unlikely persons. In this case, Pharaoh's daughter adopts Moses, a Hebrew baby, as her own son, saving him from certain death.

5 Job's friends grieve with him (Job 2:11-13).
Job has lost everything. His friends Eliphaz, Bildad, and Zophar hear of his suffering and go to comfort him. They sit with Job for seven days and nights. Good counselors, they do not speak but simply share his grief. They only mess up later when they start to talk.

6 Stephen forgives his executioners (Acts 7:54-60).
Stephen, one of the seven chosen to administer help to widows, is stoned to death because of his powerfully irritating public witness to Christ. As he is dying he asks God to forgive those who kill him.

7 The sinful woman washes Jesus' feet (Luke 7:36-50).
A woman known only as a "sinner" dares to enter a Pharisee's home where Jesus is dining. She washes Jesus' feet with her tears, dries them with her hair, and anoints his feet with ointment that costs a fortune.

TOP FIVE SIBLING RIVALRIES IN THE BIBLE

Fights between brothers and sisters are far from a new phenomenon. In fact, one might consider all such conflicts biblical.

❶ Cain and Abel (Genesis 4).
Abel was a shepherd and Cain a farmer. When God favors the "keeper of sheep" (Abel) over the "tiller of the ground" (Cain), Cain invites Abel to a field to murder his younger brother. Here begins the history of sibling squabbles—not a great precedent.

❷ Jacob and Esau (Genesis 27).
Issac and Rebekah had two grown sons, Esau and Jacob—twins born only minutes apart. While Esau, a hairy man, was out hunting game in anticipation of his birthright, younger brother Jacob and their own mother schemed to deceive Isaac in his old age so that Jacob might receive the birthright intended for Esau. What can you expect from two who struggled even in their mother's womb?

❸ Joseph and his brothers (Genesis 37–46).
When Joseph, the beloved son of Jacob, shared his dream of greatness with his brothers, they had had enough. They sold him to the Ishmaelites, dipped his robe in goat's blood, and tricked their distraught father into believing he had been killed. Despite this conspiracy, Jacob *does* rise to greatness in Egypt and eventually saves his family from famine.

❹ Solomon and Adonijah (1 Kings 1–2).
As King David grew old, it came time for him to name
his successor. His son Adonijah declared himself king.
But Bathsheba and the prophet Nathan worked to
put Bathsheba's son Solomon on the throne. When
Adonijah requested one of Solomon's concubines for a
wife, Solomon took the request as a threat. Solomon had
Adonijah killed and eventually becoming king.

❺ Mary and Martha (Luke 10).
When Jesus visited the house of the sisters Mary and Martha,
Martha went to great lengths to make preparations for the
guest. When Mary sat at Jesus' feet at the expense of her
chores, Martha complained to Jesus for Mary's lack of help.

*Siblings have always had a predilection to be at odds with each
other, even in the Bible. One of the most famous rivalries was
between the industrious Martha and her attentive sister, Mary,
when Jesus came to visit.*

TOP 10 ANGEL SIGHTINGS IN THE BIBLE

The term *angel* actually comes from the Greek word for "messenger." Here are 10 of the approximately 275 places in the Bible where God's special messengers are mentioned.

1 Balaam and his donkey (Numbers 22:22-35). Becoming angry at his donkey, Balaam struck it three times, after which they have a heated exchange (yes, a talking donkey). An angel shows up to see what Balaam's up to.

Angels, God's messengers, do not always appear clothed in radiant garments and singing hymns. The three that visited Abraham and Sarah as they tented near the oaks of Mamre were mysterious and indistinct, and their message was quite strange.

❷ The Annunciation (Luke 1:26-38).
God sent the angel Gabriel to Mary, a young teenager, to tell her she would bear a child who "will be called Son of the Most High." And so began Mary's life as the earthly mother of Jesus.

❸ Joseph considers divorce (Matthew 1:18-25).
On learning the news of Mary's pregnancy, fiancé Joseph was determined to break off their relationship. But an angel appeared to Joseph in a dream to explain that Mary had conceived a child by the Holy Spirit and would bear the savior of the world.

❹ The shepherds in the fields (Luke 2:8-15).
Perhaps one of the most famous angel stories, several appeared to the shepherds to announce the news of Jesus' birth: "Glory to God in the highest heaven, and on earth peace among those whom he favors!"

❺ Abraham, Sarah, and the three strangers (Genesis 18:1-15).
When three strangers appeared at Abraham and Sarah's home, Abraham ordered his servants to lavish the guests with choice food and drink. Later they discover the visitors are God's messengers sent to inform Sarah, though an old woman, that she would bear a son.

❻ The angel guarding Eden (Genesis 3:23-24).
After their fall from God's favor, Adam and Eve were ordered to leave the Garden of Eden. At the garden's entrance, God placed an angel with a twirling fiery sword to guard against their return.

❼ The empty tomb (Luke 24:1-9).
When a group of women went to anoint Jesus' crucified body, they found the tomb empty. Two angels startled them, telling the women that Jesus had risen from the dead.

❽ John of Patmos and the angel (Revelation 1:1-2).
The Lord sent an angel to John to share with him God's plan for the end of time. The book of Revelation is what was "revealed" in his vision.

❾ Female angels (Zechariah 5:9).
Angels are spirits, not humans, though they sometimes have a human form when they appear on earth. Most of the Bible's angels are described with male characteristics, although Zechariah 5:9 gives the impression that two angels had female forms.

❿ Daniel's fiery angel (Daniel 10:5-6).
Not all angels are described as having human characteristics. Daniel sees an angel wearing an assortment of jewels with a face like lightning and eyes like torches.

FIVE MOST COMMON IMAGES FOR GOD IN THE BIBLE

Descriptions of God in the Bible are so many as to make a complete compilation too lengthy for this little book, as are the various names for God, but there are at least five images common enough to mention as standouts.

❶ Father.
God is depicted as the father of the nation Israel (Exodus 4:22-23) and Jesus calls God "Abba! Father" (Mark 14:36).

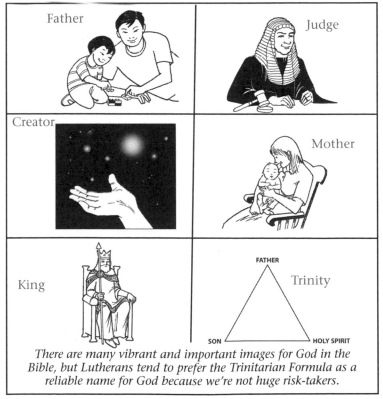

Father

Judge

Creator

Mother

King

FATHER

Trinity

SON   HOLY SPIRIT

There are many vibrant and important images for God in the Bible, but Lutherans tend to prefer the Trinitarian Formula as a reliable name for God because we're not huge risk-takers.

② Creator.

God's act of creating the universe and everything in it (Genesis 1–2) is arguably God's defining characteristic (in many psalms). In other words, to be God is to be one who creates.

③ King.

God tried to talk Israel out of demanding a king, saying, "I am ... your King" (Isaiah 43:15). God is called the power behind every throne (1 Samuel 16:13). Jesus turned the title on its head by making the cross his throne and wearing a crown of thorns.

④ Judge.

In one of Jesus' clearest teachings about what God will do at the end of time, he says that God will judge people on the basis of how we have treated one another (Matthew 25:31-46).

⑤ Mother.

Images of care giving, nurture, and love that make us think of mothers are often used for God's interactions with human beings (Isaiah 66:12-13) and Jesus uses the imagery of a mother hen (Luke 13:34) to describe his relationship to his people.

Be Aware

- Because of the superabundance of distinct images and names for God in the Bible, many people avoid adhering to a single one for too long at a stretch, referring to God in many ways. Others stick with a single name or referent for God their whole lives.
- The Trinitarian Formula accepted by Lutherans, "Father, Son, and Holy Spirit," is most commonly used in worship and is often regarded as God's name.
- Regardless of the name you use to refer to God, the Second Commandment still applies.

TOP FIVE "OTHER GODS" IN THE OLD TESTAMENT AND WHO BELIEVED IN THEM

The Old Testament is filled with warnings to the Israelites—usually ignored—against worshiping "other gods."

❶ Baal Hadad (occurs frequently in the Old Testament).
The great Canaanite god of storm and fertility. Baal gave the Lord some serious competition among the Lord's people. Ahab, for example, built an altar for Baal in Samaria in Israel, and Manasseh did the same in Jerusalem. Baal Hadad is usually depicted holding lightning bolts in his hands, prepared to strike.

❷ Asherah (Jeremiah 7:17-18).
A Canaanite mother-goddess. Like the Canaanites, Hebrews erected and worshiped carved poles representing her. Some Israelites even believed she was God's companion. The prophets repeatedly condemned the worship of Asherah.

❸ Astarte (Jeremiah 7:16-20; 44:15-19).
Originally a Canaanite war-goddess worshiped by the Philistines (1 Samuel 31:10). Astarte was probably associated with the Jerusalem "Queen of Heaven" cult against which Jeremiah preached.

❹ Dagon (1 Samuel 5:1-7).
The Philistines are said to have built temples for the warrior god Dagon, although none have yet been found. It is not known whether Dagon was a god related to a "fish man" or a god of grain.

⑤ Molech (1 Kings 11:5, 33).

A Canaanite god of fire also worshiped in Assyria. Sacrifices to Molech involved passing children through fire. Solomon was condemned for building a high place to Molech. This god had a sanctuary just south of Jerusalem.

Molech, the Canaanite god of fire, is one of the lesser-known gods in the Bible and doesn't get much press. He is sometimes called "Milcom" in the Old Testament.

HOW TO IDENTIFY AN ANGEL

The word *angel* means "messenger" in both the Hebrew of the Old Testament and the Greek of the New Testament. In the Bible, God uses angels to communicate with people—to advise, call, protect, warn, judge, kill, bless, instruct, comfort, make birth announcements, and bring good news to them. When an angel shows up, somebody is in for an awe-inspiring, bone-rattling, life-changing experience. Here's how to be sure you're dealing with the real thing.

1 Try to determine whether God might send an angel in those specific circumstances or whether you might be imagining things.
Finding a lost wallet and someone opening a door for you when you have your arms full probably don't qualify as angelic encounters. Be careful not to diminish an angel's work in your life by confusing it with made-up encounters or attributing everyday coincidences or kindnesses to an angel.

2 Listen for a godly message.
In the Bible, God almost never sends an angel without sending a message. Keep in mind that God's messages sometimes include judgment and wrath as well as comfort, grace, and healing. Look also for prophecies of impending future events.

3 Discern which type of angel you might be dealing with.
- *Old Testament angels:* Encounters with these angels are sometimes bizarre and even hazardous, but also occasionally playful. You might get your hip knocked out of its socket (Genesis 32:25) or your foot crushed (Numbers 22:25), but you might also receive good culinary advice (Judges 6:20) or protection from hungry lions (Daniel 6:22).

- **New Testament angels:** These messengers appear chiefly to deliver good news and don't seem to get too involved in matters physically, though they reserve the right to do so when necessary (Matthew 28:2; John 5:4).
- **Modern-day angels:** These angels seem to bring primarily feelings of happiness, protection, and preservation, though very seldom a message. The discrepancy with the biblical models has caused some to question the authenticity of some modern-day encounters.

❹ Take time to grapple with your angelic encounter before making final judgments and announcing it to everyone.
If it truly was an angelic encounter, God will make that clear over time, perhaps even sending the angel for repeat visits until you get the message. If not, blabbing about a questionable event might make you look like a kook.

Be Aware

- Avoid confusing an angel with God. Angels sometimes appear subtly and slip into roles the Bible attributes only to God. Angels cannot deliver salvation, grace, or forgiveness of sins.
- Hunches, intuition, and a "sixth sense" are not signs of an angelic message from God. If an angel brings a message, you'll know it.
- Angels are not believed to use telepathy, coincidence, or other cryptic signals to communicate, as in some modern-day reports. God-sent angels typically speak their messages out loud.

How to Identify an Angel

Angels are thought to perambulate by wing power.

Angels typically deliver messages verbally.

When in repose among the heavenly host, angels are thought to play harps or lyres.

Angels occasionally use their hands in their work (Matthew 4:6).

An angel's feet are considered blessed (Isaiah 52:7).

Angels' robes are white, symbolizing purity (John 20:12). Angels occasionally appear clad in other things (Revelation 10:1).

Angels often blast trumpets preceding an important announcement (Revelation 8:2).

THE FIVE MOST UNPOPULAR OLD TESTAMENT PROPHETS

New Testament tax collectors weren't alone in being hated by God's people. Here are five notorious bearers of God's message and what made them so unpopular.

1 Amos.
Amos gained few friends when he told the Israelites that their privilege came with responsibility. He prophesied against Israel's enemies and then showed Israel's practices were actually worse than the nations they hated. He even said that Israel would be destroyed. Amos let God's people know that God hates violence and oppression of the weak—no matter who's doing it.

2 Nahum.
Nahum told God's people that even a mighty army wouldn't keep a nation safe from God's judgment. About 150 years earlier, Jonah had told the Ninevites to repent (and they did), but they quickly returned to old ways. God gave Nahum a new message of destruction for the Ninevites, but they weren't scared because they had a strong army. So while the city was falling, Nahum ridiculed them by suggesting they draw water (in the midst of a flood), and add bricks to the already demolished city wall.

3 Micah.
Micah told the people that God wants disciples to have humble hearts and behavior that is just and kind to others. He said God would come and destroy the nation of Judah because the powerful had schemed to steal from the poor and followed false prophets. They thought following ritual was enough. It wasn't.

❹ Zephaniah.

Zephaniah was another prophet in Judah. He made his enemies by warning that even those who refused to worship idols would face God's judgment because they didn't follow God.

❺ Jeremiah.

God called Jeremiah to be a prophet when he was just a boy. This gave him more time to confront God's people about their self-focused lives. He was persecuted bitterly by Judah's last two kings—and even his own extended family tried to kill him. Jeremiah's messages were many—but this one still speaks: Those who are godly may suffer persecution, but they should look to God for salvation!

The Lord's prophets tended to be unpopular, especially among the wealthy, because their messages called for justice toward others and fidelity toward God. Amos was particularly unpopular for this reason.

FIVE INSPIRING WOMEN IN THE BIBLE

There are more than 300 women mentioned in the Bible. Some have names, others are referred to as "the women" or some other similar designation. Theologians and scholars have begun to highlight the lives of these many women and speak of their contributions to the story of God. Here are a few of the more inspiring examples.

❶ **Miriam, Jochebed, Puah, Shiphrah, and Pharaoh's daughter.**
These five women were instrumental in the survival of Moses. Without their quick thinking, strong courage, and love of God, Moses would have drowned in the Nile River along with many other baby boys. *Note: We are naming more than one woman in this instance, but that's fine. It's a single story that involves them all.*

❷ **Ruth.**
Ruth chose not to return to her homeland and family after the death of her husband in order to attend to the needs of her mother-in-law, Naomi. Ruth showed intelligence and compassion in gaining the security she and Naomi needed upon their return to Israel. Other women in the story even remarked that Ruth was more valuable than having a son—a high compliment in those days of male preference.

❸ **Esther.**
When an evil man threatened to annihilate her people, Queen Esther used her beauty and skills in negotiation to save them. Esther is commemorated each year during Purim, a Jewish holiday.

❹ Lydia.

Lydia was known as a God fearer, a follower of God who regularly prayed with her household. She began a house church and attended to the needs of the apostle Paul. Her house may have been the first European Christian congregation.

❺ Mary, the Mother of the Lord.

At a young age, Mary answered a resounding "YES" to the angel's request that she bear God's Son.

Lydia was a "God fearer," someone who received the gospel of Jesus Christ and was used to spread the good news in her town.

TOP FIVE MISCONCEPTIONS ABOUT THE BOOK OF REVELATION

The book of Revelation is among the most misunderstood—and misused—books in all written literature. In fact, some people make a good living misinterpreting Revelation for others with apocalyptic fiction. Lutherans, however, enjoy debunking these myths.

❶ The author of Revelation was John, the disciple of Jesus, son of Zebedee.
The writer's name was John (a common New Testament name), but not John the apostle. In chapter 21, he refers to "the twelve" with no hint that he was one of them.

❷ Combining Revelation with other biblical end-time references reveals a hidden schedule for Christ's return.
Many rapture theories take verses from Daniel, Matthew, 1 and 2 Thessalonians, and 1 John and combine them with parts of Revelation to construct their apocalyptic scenarios. This treats the Bible like a box of puzzle pieces. It's better to read Revelation on its own, as a whole book with integrity and unity.

❸ Revelation is only about the future.
Revelation is not a future history of the end of the world, or a mysterious, coded prediction that will only be understood later. It is a letter written to be read to first-century Christian churches. "John to the seven churches that are in Asia" (Revelation 1:4). Revelation's message would have been pretty clearly understood by its original hearers.

4 Revelation is only about the past.

Much of the letter is probably symbolic of imperial Rome. However, there is also much in it about God's future salvation for the world. Plus, what Revelation teaches about remaining faithful and hopeful in a faithless and challenging world speaks to all Christians today.

5 Revelation is just too weird to hear read out loud in worship.

On the contrary, much of our liturgy comes from Revelation, as well as the words of many favorite hymns, including "Holy, Holy, Holy," "Alabare," "Who Is This Host Arrayed in White," "For All the Saints," and "Shall We Gather at the River?"

Be Aware

- The book is not called "Revelations," with an "s," as many people incorrectly say, but Revelation. No "s" at the end, please.
- The return of Christ cannot be ignored; it is a crucial part of our faith. When we say the Apostles' Creed we confess, "He will come again to judge the living and the dead."

Among the most common misconceptions about the book of Revelation is the idea that it is plural.

HOW TO TELL WHEN THE APOCALYPSE IS IMMINENT

There has been a great deal of best-selling speculation about the Apocalypse—Christ's Second Coming. Here's what to look for—or *not* look for, as the case may be—based on what Jesus said.

❶ It'll be mostly invisible to the naked eye.
"The kingdom of God is not coming with things that can be observed," said Jesus (Luke 17:20). Don't rely on television coverage or newspaper headlines for signs.

❷ People will simply go about their daily business.
When the End is near, people will eat and drink, buy and sell, plant and build, marry, and so on (Luke 17:27-28). It will be "business as usual."

❸ Some Christians will be in for a rough time.
Jesus' followers will suffer like he did, and will testify to their faith (Luke 21:12).

❹ It will be difficult to distinguish it from other days.
There will be wars, earthquakes, famines, plagues, and unrest in the Middle East (Luke 21:20-24).

❺ Prophets and false prophets will rise.
Some people will claim that they see signs of Jesus' coming (Luke 21:25-27).

Be Aware

- When asked what he would do if he knew the world would end tomorrow, Martin Luther said he would plant a tree today. To expect Christ's coming is not to live in fear, but in the joyful expectation that "your redemption is drawing near" (Luke 21:28).

When asked what he would do if he knew the world would end tomorrow, Martin Luther said he would plant a tree today. To expect Christ's coming again is not to live in fear but in joyful expectation.

HOW TO LOCATE THE "CANON WITHIN THE CANON"

The term *canon* comes from the Latin word for "standard" or "rule" or "measuring line." With respect to the Scriptures, figuring out which books made it into the canon of the Bible was a long, difficult process of defining the standard and then measuring the dozens of writings against it. Martin Luther raised the standard even higher, claiming that certain books within the Bible are a "canon within the canon," based on what—or *who*—they preached.

❶ Get fitted for a pair of Jesus glasses.
Locating the canon within the canon requires sight tuned to Christ's wavelength. You'll know you've hit upon it when a book or passage preaches both God's law and freedom in Jesus Christ.

❷ Avoid pretending you hold all parts of the Bible as equals.
Everyone has his or her own canon within the canon. Lutherans are just upfront about theirs.

❸ Remain open to books that preach God's law and reveal Christ's gospel. Don't worry so much about the others.
The uniquely Lutheran idea of "canon within the canon" says that not only some passages but also entire books of the Bible are central, and therefore other passages and books are not. Many Lutheran die-hards insist that the canon within the canon finds *you* more than you can find *it*.

❹ Discern the central message of a book as you read it.
For Lutherans, this message is that God graciously forgives
sinful people through faith, apart from works, for the sake
of Jesus Christ. Avoid the common mistake of believing
that the canon within the canon does not include the law.

❺ Start with the books you know fit the profile.
Martin Luther wrote, "In a word St. John's Gospel and his
first epistle, St. Paul's epistles, especially Romans, Galatians,
and Ephesians, and St. Peter's first epistle are the books
that show you Christ and teach you all that is necessary
for you to know, even if you were never to see or hear any
other book or doctrine" (*Luther's Works* 35:362).

Jesus' face

*Locating the "canon within the canon" in the Bible requires a
pair of Jesus glasses, because for Lutherans the Bible is at its best
when it reveals both God's law and freedom in Jesus Christ.*

HOW TO LISTEN TO SCRIPTURE AS IT IS READ ALOUD AND GET SOMETHING OUT OF IT

Lutheran theologians agree that "faith comes through hearing," and that a sharp ear for law and gospel is a key tool for those who follow Jesus Christ and can enrich one's experience of "dwelling in the Word richly."

As you listen to a passage read aloud, consider highlighting key sentences for further investigation or inquiry. Tracking in this way can help you focus and get more out of the Bible.

❶ Prepare your mind to engage the reading.
This is especially important if you don't have the words in front of you. Settle yourself, breathe deeply, and listen closely. You might say the words quietly in your head right after the reader speaks. If you know you won't doze, consider closing your eyes to "visualize" the reading in you mind's eye.

❷ Consider placing a copy of the text in front of you.
Your church worship folder (or bulletin) may include the scripture for the day. Your sanctuary may have a Bible in the pew rack. Or even better, bring your own Bible to worship.

❸ Highlight important words and words of interest. Review later.
Physically tracking the words as they are read and capturing the phrases that pique your curiosity can facilitate understanding.

❹ Create and use a personalized system of editor's marks.
Use symbols to indicate questions, words of praise, promises, or other ideas. Write those symbols in the margins of your Bible or on the bulletin. Please do not write in the pew Bibles.

❺ Sharpen active listening through the ancient spiritual practice of *lectio divina*.
"Enter" the biblical text by listening for a particular phrase that jumps out to you. Concentrate on that one phrase; meditate on it.

❻ Increase your retention by reading or rereading the passage later at home.
Incorporate the reading into your daily devotions through-out the week and continue to pray and meditate on it.

SEVEN IMPORTANT BIBLE TEACHINGS EVERY LUTHERAN SHOULD KNOW

The Lutheran tradition, which takes its name from a Bible teacher who did his job with profound thoroughness, has always centered its conversations and proclamations in the Bible. At minimum, a basic understanding of these passages can help keep you on track.

1 The Bible is the written and inspired Word of God (2 Timothy 3:16).
The Bible records and announces God's redemption in Jesus and God's presence through the Holy Spirit (Hebrews 4:12). The Bible is the authoritative source and norm of the church's proclamation, faith, and life.

2 There is one God (Deuteronomy 6:4).
Our one God exists in three persons: the Father, the Son, and the Holy Spirit (Matthew 3:16-17; 28:19). This One God existed before the beginning of the world (Genesis 1:1-3) and has sent Jesus as our true way of salvation (John 3:16).

3 Jesus Christ is Lord and Savior (Colossians 1:15-20).
Jesus was completely human and completely divine. He asks us to believe in our hearts and confess with our lips that he is our Lord and Savior (Romans 10:8-9). Jesus is God Incarnate, who offers us salvation by God's grace through faith for good works (Ephesians 2:8-10).

❹ The Holy Spirit is the indwelling presence of God (John 20:22).
The Holy Spirit convicts us of sin (Romans 3:21-23) but also promises regeneration and salvation for all who believe (Romans 3:24-26). Lutherans believe that the Holy Spirit calls, gathers, enlightens, and keeps the whole Christian church on earth.

❺ Jesus instituted Holy Baptism and the Lord's Supper (Matthew 3:13-17; 26:26-29).
The sacraments are called the *means of grace*. Along with our faith, the sacraments are effective and essential for our salvation (Mark 16:16). Through the sacraments and the spoken Word, we experience regeneration in the Holy Spirit (Titus 3:5-8).

❻ The church is an inclusive fellowship (Ephesians 4:4-6).
The church gathers for worship, witness, and service (Romans 15:7). Through the proclamation of the Word and the administration of the sacraments, the church carries out the creative, redeeming, and sanctifying mission of God in the world (Matthew 28:16-20).

❼ Christ will one day return in power to judge the living and the dead (Matthew 25:31ff).
It is the privilege of believers to be assured of their salvation and to live daily in the light of Christ's love (Romans 13:11-14).

Be Aware

- These seven teachings do not constitute *everything* a Lutheran should be familiar with about the Bible, but they're a very good start.

TEN COMMON OCCUPATIONS IN BIBLE TIMES

❶ Shepherd.
Shepherds had a mixed reputation, as they worked far from home and were unable to keep many of the ritual laws. Israel's most famous king, David, was discovered while tending his father's sheep. Lamb was the most common entrée of the day.

❷ Servant/Slave.
Servants provided household duties and provided menial labor. Israel's release from slavery in Egypt is remembered as the saving event in Exodus. As a model for his followers, Jesus acted as a servant when washing the disciples' feet. At Jesus' time, roughly one-third of the region's population was enslaved.

Perhaps the most common occupation in the Bible is that of shepherd.

❸ Water gatherer.
Women typically gathered the household water each day, carrying jugs in the early morning and evening. Isaac's servant discovered Rebekah as she came with a jug of water, and Jesus revealed himself as Messiah to the Samaritan woman at the well.

❹ Fisherman.
Fish put food on the table and provided a source of income. Jesus called his first disciples, Peter, Andrew, James, and John, from their boats on the Sea of Galilee.

❺ Farmer/Vintner.
Agriculture was the basis for the economy in the Bible. Crops included olives, wheat, barley, dates, grapes, and figs. Jesus used many farming and wine-based images in his teachings.

A third of the region's population was enslaved during Jesus' time, which is why it's such a common occupation in the Bible.

❻ Priest.

Priests served as mediators between God and the people in rituals of prayer and sacrifice. During the time of the temple, they ensured that the laws governing worship were carried out. Zechariah was keeping the oil lamps lit when after scaring him, the angel announced the birth of his son, John the Baptist.

❼ Judge.

Judges were assembled once Israel was formed into tribes before the time of kings. They were like chieftains that resolved disputes and even fought battles. Famous judges include Deborah, Gideon, and Samson.

The climate in Bible lands is ideal for growing grapes, and wine was a safe, plentiful beverage. Consequently, vintner became a common occupation.

8 Prophet.
Prophets were designated by kings or called directly by the Lord. They were considered the conscience of the people who spoke God's word.

9 Food preparer.
Women and servants spent much of the day in food-related tasks. Sarah prepared barley cakes for the three strangers visiting at Mamre. And Martha was working in the kitchen while Mary was learning from Jesus.

10 King.
Kings were responsible for Israel's well-being and faithfulness to God. Israel's first king was Saul, followed by David. David's son Solomon was the wealthiest of all the kings and built the first temple.

TOP 10 PRAYERS UTTERED IN THE BIBLE

OLD TESTAMENT

1 Abraham's prayer for Sodom (Genesis 18:16-33).
Abraham's prayer on behalf of the people of Sodom focuses on the character of God rather than on the inhospitality and sin of the people of Sodom.

2 Moses' prayer for Israel in the wilderness (Exodus 32:9-14).
In this momentous prayer, Moses changed the mind of God from the destruction God had planned. Moses' prayer preserved the people of Israel.

3 Solomon's prayer of dedication of the temple (2 Chronicles 6:1—7:4).
Solomon praised God for being present in the temple and on the earth among sinful people. This prayer of dedication and praise gives profound thanks to God.

4 David's psalm of surrender (Psalm 139).
After coming face to face with God's intimate knowledge of him even in his mother's womb, David offers a prayer of surrender to God's searching, knowing, and refining ways.

5 Daniel's confession on behalf of his people (Daniel 9:1-19).
Daniel pleads with God to bring his people to their land even though they had rebelled. His hope was that God would be merciful and that the people would be deeply thankful.

Paul's prayer for the Ephesians, among the most profound and beautiful in all of Scripture, proves that it doesn't hurt to write things down.

NEW TESTAMENT

❻ The Lord's Prayer (Matthew 6:5-15).
Jesus' teaching on prayer includes the Lord's Prayer as a pattern of being able to go to God with our needs, our struggles, and our praise.

❼ Jesus' prayer for his disciples (John 17:1-26).
Often called "The High Priestly Prayer," this wonderful prayer emphasizes that eternal life comes by knowing God through Jesus Christ. Jesus prays that his followers be one, just as he, the Father, and the Holy Spirit are One.

8 Jesus' prayer in the Garden of Gethsemane (Matthew 26:36-45).

Jesus' agony in the garden helps us know that he experienced the depth of human suffering, but his commitment was to leave his life in God's hands.

9 Paul's prayer for the Ephesians (Ephesians 1:15-23; 3:14-21).

In this magnificent prayer Paul prays for the Ephesians to comprehend and embrace the heights and depths of God's amazing grace and love.

10 The prayer of the great multitude (Revelation 19:1-10).

At the heart of worship is praise. This prayer, from the end of the Bible, is the triumphant roar of a great multitude in praise and worship.

TOP 10 CURSES UTTERED IN THE BIBLE

A curse is a spoken formula intended to bring misfortune to its recipient. Curses are uttered often in the Bible and it is correct to assume that they are meant as punishment. However, at times God's grace stows away on these malediction—and once judgment has done its work, God steps in to redeem those who had once been cursed.

Note: Please read these curses in your Bible so that you may view them in their entirety and context.

❶ "In pain you shall bring forth children, ... cursed is the ground because of you; in toil you shall eat of it all the days of your life" (Genesis 3:16-17).
After pronouncing the first curse to the naked and shivering earthlings God sat down to sew the couple their first outfits.

❷ "I will give your flesh to the birds of the air and to the wild animals of the field" (1 Samuel 17:44).
Goliath mocked the shepherd boy who came to fight him. This hollow curse didn't come to fruition since Goliath spoke it in the name of his false gods.

❸ "I will strike you down and cut off your head" (1 Samuel 17:46).
David matched Goliath's curse and raised it with decapitation. This curse was effective because David made it in the name of the God of Israel, who is true.

Before

After

There are many nasty curses in the Bible. A hungry Jesus cursed the fig tree that bore no fruit, scaring the heck out of all the other fig trees.

❹ "May the LORD avenge me on you; but my hand shall not be against you!" (1 Samuel 24:12).
Saul sought to kill David, who had defeated Goliath. But David lay a hand on Saul because he knew that it had been God, not he, who had beaten Goliath.

❺ Elisha "cursed them in the name of the LORD. Then two she-bears came out of the woods and mauled forty-two of the boys" (2 Kings 2:23-25).
Some say this was a gang of thugs threatening Elisha, in which case it was good to have God on his side.

⑥ "After this Job opened his mouth and cursed the day of his birth. Job said: 'Let the day perish on which I was born!'" (Job 3:1-3).
While his curse was lengthy and poetic, it was the first good thing that happened to Job. His curse didn't take hold and God redeemed him.

⑦ "You son of the devil, you enemy of all righteousness, ... the hand of the LORD is against you, and you will be blind for a while, unable to see the sun" (Acts 13:10-11).
Receive God's grace; don't keep it from others. This curse was for someone who did just that.

⑧ "May your silver perish with you, because you thought you could obtain God's gift with money!" (Acts 8:20).
This curse was made against a magician who was so amazed by God's power and grace that he attempted to purchase and own it. God's grace is free, however, totally free.

⑨ "Seeing a fig tree by the side of the road, he went to it and found nothing at all on it but leaves. Then he said to it, 'May no fruit ever come from you again!' And the fig tree withered at once" (Matthew 21:18-20).
Jesus usually preferred not to curse people, but fruitless trees were basically out of luck.

⑩ "Then he began to curse, and he swore an oath, 'I do not know the man!'" (Matthew 26:74).
Peter's curse was meant to create a distance between himself and Jesus. Luckily for him, there is no place you can go where Jesus can't reach. The risen Christ found and forgave him.

A BRIEF HISTORY OF GOD'S COVENANT WITH THE PEOPLE

A covenant is a solemn exchange of promises between two parties. Five main biblical covenants reveal the history of God's relationship with the people, and these covenants often included signs. God always keeps promises, even though people rarely do.

❶ Covenant with Noah.
Because of human evil, God threatened to destroy human life with a great flood. But God repented of that intention and saved humanity through Noah and his family. God then entered into a covenant with all living creatures and promised never again to destroy life on earth with a flood. As a sign of this promise, God put the rainbow in the sky.

❷ Covenant with Abraham and Sarah.
God entered into a covenant with Abraham and Sarah so that their descendants would be "blessed to be a blessing." God promised that they would have many descendants and that the people would have a land to live in. As a sign of this promise, male Hebrew babies are circumcised.

❸ Covenant with Moses and all Israel.
After delivering the people from slavery in Egypt, God entered into a covenant with them. The Lord promised to be their God, and the people promised to be God's people. As part of the covenant, God gave the people the Ten Commandments and restored them to the land. As a sign of this covenant, God gave the Sabbath—one day off each week to rest from work and to spend time with God.

❹ Covenant with David.

David decided to build God a temple. God said, "No, I will build you a house," meaning a family tree. God promised King David that one of his descendants would forever rule over the people.

Interlude: The Promise of a New Covenant.
People are sinners. They did not keep the promises that they had made as part of their covenants with God. So through prophets such as Jeremiah and Ezekiel, God promised to make a new covenant.

❺ The New Covenant.

On the night in which he was betrayed, Jesus Christ made the new covenant. Through his death and resurrection, Jesus forgave all people for their sins and opened the way to eternal life for all. Through baptism, we become members of this covenant. Through Holy Communion, we are nourished in the covenant. The signs of the covenant are water, bread, and wine.

HOW TO READ KEY TYPES OF BIBLE LITERATURE

Like a newspaper, the Bible contains different types of writing gathered together in a single place. When reading a newspaper, readers make a mental adjustment based on the kind of material they're reading. You do not read the funnies the same way you read an advice column or a news story. The same thing goes for reading the Bible.

GENERAL GUIDELINES.

- **Clarify the unclear bits first.**
  One challenge of reading a Bible passage is to understand what it says on a basic level. Does the passage contain ancient terms or refer to ancient social practices that need clarification? Get the information clear before proceeding to higher meanings. Glossing over them will reduce the opportunity for God's word to reach you later on.

- **Ask of every passage you read, "What does this mean?"**
  After clarifying exactly what a passage says, probe the meaning of the passage. Lutherans take their Bible reading cues from Martin Luther himself, a Bible scholar who demanded the highest standards of understanding for himself.

Like a newspaper, the Bible contains different types of writing gathered together in a single place.

A Psalm.

- **Discern which type of psalm it is, then read it accordingly.**

  A psalm is always a poem and is often a prayer. If the psalm is a prayer, read it as a prayer—words spoken to God. To the extent that the prayer fits your life, make it your own. For parts that do not fit your life, pray the prayer on behalf of other people.

- **Open yourself up to the psalm's teaching.**

  The psalms are also poems of instruction; they teach us about God and ourselves. Explore the psalm as a poem, teasing out the meaning of its metaphors (such as God is a rock, or we are like trees) for your own life.

A Prophetic Message.
The prophets were not predictors or prognosticators. They were messengers from God who brought God's word to specific times and places.

- **Learn the historical background.**
  When reading a prophetic message, learn what you can about the time, place, and people to whom the message was sent (the notes in a good study Bible can help you do this). Learn what was going on that led God to send a message.

- **Apply the prophet's message to your own life.**
  After understanding God's message as fully as possible, apply that message to yourself, your time, and your people.

A Parable.
A parable is a short story designed to make a point. Jesus often used parables to teach and preach, often with a very specific message to a very specific audience.

- **Discern the original audience.**
  When reading a parable, pay attention to whom Jesus addressed the parable. Was he telling the story to his disciples, or was he addressing his religious or political opponents? Keep this in mind when applying the story to yourself and your own time.

- **Balance Jesus' message from one parable with other lessons you learn.**
  What you learn from a parable is just one of the many lessons available in the Bible. Be wary about drawing too big of a conclusion from just one parable.

A Letter.

- **Engage in active eavesdropping.**
  When you read a letter (sometimes called an epistle), remember that you are reading someone else's mail. It is a little like listening in to one part of a phone conversation.

- **Avoid taking a portion out of context (known among Bible geeks as "proof-texting"). Use caution.**
  In order to understand the part of the conversation you're reading, you have to work to place the little part of the conversation that you are overhearing within the larger conversation. Taking that smaller portion out of context can lead to all kinds of bad results.

A Narrative Account.

- **Always take the big picture into account.**
  When reading a portion of a narrative, try to place the part of the story that you are reading within the larger narrative. It is important to acknowledge that, as a reader, you know things about what is happening "behind the scenes" or about the ending of the story that the people in the story don't know yet.

- **Keep in mind who says what.**
  If Jesus says something, you can bet it is true. But if the devil or a sinner says something, it may or may not be true.

A Proverb.

Proverbs are short, wise sayings meant to teach a practical lesson. There is a book of Proverbs in the Old Testament, but proverbs show up in other places too.

- **Take it for what it's worth.**
  Proverbs often teach very practical things about daily life. They're not meant, however, to become slogans or personal mission statements that take over your life.

- **Consider memorizing proverbs you find meaningful for your life.**
  Proverbs can add clarity in certain moments along the path. You may find the ones you memorize carry a theme that is particular to your situation or personality.

HOW TO INTERPRET "CONTROVERSIAL" BIBLE TEXTS AND REMAIN LUTHERAN

The Bible is filled with passages that are difficult to interpret or that people use in controversial ways. (The U.S. Supreme Court once used the Bible in a legal argument to defend and support slavery, for example.) Lutheran Christians inherit from our forebears some handy methods of figuring out how God is speaking to us through the Bible about tough contemporary issues, all while keeping our wits about us and the focus on Jesus Christ.

❶ Distinguish the *law* from the gospel within the passage.
One of the very first Lutheran documents says, "All Scripture should be divided into … the law and the promises."

- **The law:** The law is what God tells us to do for ourselves and for each other. Example: Love your neighbor.
- **The promise:** The promise, or gospel, is what God promises to do for us, because we cannot do it for ourselves. Example: Attain eternal life.
- **Which one?** We get into trouble when we confuse the two. When we expect God to do for us what God tells us to do (love your neighbor) or when we try to do for ourselves what only God can do for us (grant eternal life), we miss the mark.

❷ Ask whether the passage in question delivers Christ. Lutherans believe the Scriptures have authority because they "preach and inculcate [deliver] Christ. And this is the true test by which we judge all books, when we see whether they inculcate [deliver] Christ."

- **Delivering the true Christ:** Christ so loved the world that he laid down his life to save us. Is the passage being used by someone for some means other than preaching Christ as the savior of the world?
- **Let love be your guide:** Ask what a loving use of the Scripture passage would look like.

Some passages in the Bible can be controversial and difficult to comprehend in light of current events. Lutherans rely on their special method of carefully distinguishing the law from the gospel to make sense of things.

❸ Test the passage to see whether it is about us, today. The Bible is filled with stories of God's people in different places and times. People sometimes pull a passage out of context and act as if God spoke the word through the radio today.

- For all times and places? Ask if the passage is a message for all times and places.
- **Sometimes "yes":** Sometimes passages do apply *directly* to us today. When Jesus says to love the Lord with all our hearts and love our neighbors as ourselves (Matthew 22:37-39), it is a good bet God means all of us all the time.
- **Sometimes "no":** Sometimes, passages apply *indirectly* to us today. Deuteronomy says, "When you build a new house, you shall make a parapet for your roof; otherwise you might bear bloodguilt on your house, if anyone should fall from it" (22:8), and it's a good bet that we need to apply this to our lives *indirectly*. But we do apply it to our lives.

❹ Attempt to discern the original context of the passage; avoid cobbling together a fractured message from discrete parts of the Bible.
Often, people connect the dots between very different passages and create a crazy line drawing.

- **Context, Part 1:** Figure out the context of the passage. Does reading the passage in its context help to clarify its meaning? If someone strings together more than one passage, are they using the different passages in a way that is faithful to original contexts?

- **Context, Part 2:** Figure out the context in which we are today. Are you using an ancient passage to support something in our culture that is contrary to God's will? Is there some sacred cow you are protecting by the use of this Scripture?

Be Aware
- Lutherans believe strongly in a shared interpretation of the Bible. This means we tend to prefer figuring out what the Bible means for our time *together*, in conversation and honest debate, rather than simply allowing disagreements to resolve into conflict.
- Sometimes disagreements about the Bible can endure for long periods of time before events catch up.

SMALL CATECHISM OF MARTIN LUTHER

As printed in *Evangelical Lutheran Worship*

THE TEN COMMANDMENTS

The First Commandment

You shall have no other gods.

What is this? or *What does this mean?*
We are to fear, love, and trust God above all things.

The Second Commandment

You shall not make wrongful use of the name of the Lord your God.

What is this? or *What does this mean?*
We are to fear and love God, so that we do not curse, swear, practice magic, lie, or deceive using God's name, but instead use that very name in every time of need to call on, pray to, praise, and give thanks to God.

The Third Commandment

Remember the sabbath day, and keep it holy.

What is this? or *What does this mean?*
We are to fear and love God, so that we do not despise preaching or God's word, but instead keep that word holy and gladly hear and learn it.

The Fourth Commandment

Honor your father and your mother.

What is this? or *What does this mean?*
We are to fear and love God, so that we neither despise nor anger our parents and others in authority, but instead honor, serve, obey, love, and respect them.

The Fifth Commandment

You shall not murder.

What is this? or *What does this mean?*
We are to fear and love God, so that we neither endanger nor harm the lives of our neighbors, but instead help and support them in all of life's needs.

The Sixth Commandment

You shall not commit adultery.

What is this? or *What does this mean?*
We are to fear and love God, so that we lead pure and decent lives in word and deed, and each of us loves and honors his or her spouse.

The Seventh Commandment

You shall not steal.

What is this? or *What does this mean?*
We are to fear and love God, so that we neither take our neighbors' money or property nor acquire them by using shoddy merchandise or crooked deals, but instead help them to improve and protect their property and income.

The Eighth Commandment

You shall not bear false witness against your neighbor.

What is this? or *What does this mean?*
We are to fear and love God, so that we do not tell lies about our neighbors, betray or slander them, or destroy their reputations. Instead we are to come to their defense, speak well of them, and interpret everything they do in the best possible light.

The Ninth Commandment
You shall not covet your neighbor's house.

What is this? or *What does this mean?*
We are to fear and love God, so that we do not try to trick our neighbors out of their inheritance or property or try to get it for ourselves by claiming to have a legal right to it and the like, but instead be of help and service to them in keeping what is theirs.

The Tenth Commandment
You shall not covet your neighbor's wife, or male or female slave, or ox, or donkey, or anything that belongs to your neighbor.

What is this? or *What does this mean?*
We are to fear and love God, so that we do not entice, force, or steal away from our neighbors their spouses, household workers, or livestock, but instead urge them to stay and fulfill their responsibilities to our neighbors.

What then does God say about all these commandments?
God says the following: "I, the Lord your God, am a jealous God, punishing children for the iniquity of parents, to the third and the fourth generation of those who reject me, but showing steadfast love to the thousandth generation of those who love me and keep my commandments."

What is this? or *What does this mean?*
God threatens to punish all who break these commandments. Therefore we are to fear his wrath and not disobey these commandments. However, God promises grace and every good thing to all those who keep these commandments. Therefore we also are to love and trust him and gladly act according to his commands.

THE CREED

The First Article: On Creation

 I believe in God, the Father almighty, creator of heaven and earth.

 What is this? or *What does this mean?*
I believe that God has created me together with all that exists. God has given me and still preserves my body and soul: eyes, ears, and all limbs and senses; reason and all mental faculties.

 In addition, God daily and abundantly provides shoes and clothing, food and drink, house and farm, spouse and children, fields, livestock, and all property—along with all the necessities and nourishment for this body and life. God protects me against all danger and shields and preserves me from all evil. And all this is done out of pure, fatherly, and divine goodness and mercy, without any merit or worthiness of mine at all! For all of this I owe it to God to thank and praise, serve and obey him. This is most certainly true.

The Second Article: On Redemption

 I believe in Jesus Christ, God's only Son, our Lord, who was conceived by the Holy Spirit, born of the virgin Mary, suffered under Pontius Pilate, was crucified, died, and was buried; he descended to the dead.* On the third day he rose again; he ascended into heaven, he is seated at the right hand of the Father, and he will come to judge the living and the dead.

*Or, "he descended into hell," another translation of this text in widespread use.

What is this? or *What does this mean?*
I believe that Jesus Christ, true God, begotten of the
Father in eternity, and also a true human being, born
of the virgin Mary, is my Lord. He has redeemed me, a
lost and condemned human being. He has purchased
and freed me from all sins, from death, and from the
power of the devil, not with gold or silver but with his
holy, precious blood and with his innocent suffering and
death. He has done all this in order that I may belong to
him, live under him in his kingdom, and serve him in
eternal righteousness, innocence, and blessedness, just
as he is risen from the dead and lives and rules eternally.
This is most certainly true.

The Third Article: On Being Made Holy

I believe in the Holy Spirit, the holy catholic church,
the communion of saints, the forgiveness of sins, the
resurrection of the body, and the life everlasting.

What is this? or *What does this mean?*
I believe that by my own understanding or strength I
cannot believe in Jesus Christ my Lord or come to him,
but instead the Holy Spirit has called me through the
gospel, enlightened me with his gifts, made me holy
and kept me in the true faith, just as he calls, gathers,
enlightens, and makes holy the whole Christian church
on earth and keeps it with Jesus Christ in the one
common, true faith. Daily in this Christian church the
Holy Spirit abundantly forgives all sins—mine and those
of all believers. On the last day the Holy Spirit will raise
me and all the dead and will give to me and all believers
in Christ eternal life. This is most certainly true.

THE LORD'S PRAYER

Introduction

Our Father in heaven.

What is this? or *What does this mean?*

With these words God wants to attract us, so that we come to believe he is truly our Father and we are truly his children, in order that we may ask him boldly and with complete confidence, just as loving children ask their loving father.

The First Petition

Hallowed be your name.

What is this? or *What does this mean?*

It is true that God's name is holy in itself, but we ask in this prayer that it may also become holy in and among us.

How does this come about?

Whenever the word of God is taught clearly and purely and we, as God's children, also live holy lives according to it. To this end help us, dear Father in heaven! However, whoever teaches and lives otherwise than the word of God teaches, dishonors the name of God among us. Preserve us from this, heavenly Father!

The Second Petition

Your kingdom come.

What is this? or *What does this mean?*

In fact, God's kingdom comes on its own without our prayer, but we ask in this prayer that it may also come to us.

How does this come about?
Whenever our heavenly Father gives us his Holy Spirit, so that through the Holy Spirit's grace we believe God's holy word and live godly lives here in time and hereafter in eternity.

The Third Petition

Your will be done, on earth as in heaven.

What is this? or *What does this mean?*
In fact, God's good and gracious will comes about without our prayer, but we ask in this prayer that it may also come about in and among us.

How does this come about?
Whenever God breaks and hinders every evil scheme and will—as are present in the will of the devil, the world, and our flesh—that would not allow us to hallow God's name and would prevent the coming of his kingdom, and instead whenever God strengthens us and keeps us steadfast in his word and in faith until the end of our lives. This is God's gracious and good will.

The Fourth Petition

Give us today our daily bread.

What is this? or *What does this mean?*
In fact, God gives daily bread without our prayer, even to all evil people, but we ask in this prayer that God cause us to recognize what our daily bread is and to receive it with thanksgiving.

What then does "daily bread" mean?
Everything included in the necessities and nourishment for our bodies, such as food, drink, clothing, shoes, house, farm, fields, livestock, money, property, an

upright spouse, upright children, upright members of the household, upright and faithful rulers, good government, good weather, peace, health, decency, honor, good friends, faithful neighbors, and the like.

The Fifth Petition

Forgive us our sins, as we forgive those who sin against us.

What is this? or *What does this mean?*
We ask in this prayer that our heavenly Father would not regard our sins nor deny these petitions on their account, for we are worthy of nothing for which we ask, nor have we earned it. Instead we ask that God would give us all things by grace, for we daily sin much and indeed deserve only punishment. So, on the other hand, we, too, truly want to forgive heartily and to do good gladly to those who sin against us.

The Sixth Petition

Save us from the time of trial.

What is this? or *What does this mean?*
It is true that God tempts no one, but we ask in this prayer that God would preserve and keep us, so that the devil, the world, and our flesh may not deceive us or mislead us into false belief, despair, and other great and shameful sins, and that, although we may be attacked by them, we may finally prevail and gain the victory.

The Seventh Petition

And deliver us from evil.

What is this? or *What does this mean?*

We ask in this prayer, as in a summary, that our Father in heaven may deliver us from all kinds of evil—affecting body or soul, property or reputation—and at last, when our final hour comes, may grant us a blessed end and take us by grace from this valley of tears to himself in heaven.

Conclusion

[For the kingdom, the power, and the glory are yours, now and forever.] Amen.

What is this? or *What does this mean?*

That I should be certain that such petitions are acceptable to and heard by our Father in heaven, for he himself commanded us to pray like this and has promised to hear us. "Amen, amen" means "Yes, yes, it is going to come about just like this."

THE SACRAMENT OF HOLY BAPTISM

I

What is baptism?
Baptism is not simply plain water. Instead, it is water used according to God's command and connected with God's word.

What then is this word of God?
Where our Lord Christ says in Matthew 28, "Go therefore and make disciples of all nations, baptizing them in the name of the Father and of the Son and of the Holy Spirit."

II

What gifts or benefits does baptism grant?
It brings about forgiveness of sins, redeems from death and the devil, and gives eternal salvation to all who believe it, as the words and promise of God declare.

What are these words and promise of God?
Where our Lord Christ says in Mark 16, "The one who believes and is baptized will be saved; but the one who does not believe will be condemned."

III

How can water do such great things?
Clearly the water does not do it, but the word of God, which is with and alongside the water, and faith, which trusts this word of God in the water. For without the word of God the water is plain water and not a baptism, but with the word of God it is a baptism, that is, a grace-filled water of life and a "bath of the new birth in

the Holy Spirit," as St. Paul says to Titus in chapter 3, "through the water of rebirth and renewal by the Holy Spirit. This Spirit he poured out on us richly through Jesus Christ our Savior, so that, having been justified by his grace, we might become heirs according to the hope of eternal life. The saying is sure."

IV

What then is the significance of such a baptism with water?
It signifies that the old person in us with all sins and evil desires is to be drowned and die through daily sorrow for sin and through repentance, and on the other hand that daily a new person is to come forth and rise up to live before God in righteousness and purity forever.

Where is this written?
St. Paul says in Romans 6, "We have been buried with Christ by baptism into death, so that, just as Christ was raised from the dead by the glory of the Father, so we too might walk in newness of life."

How people are to be taught to confess

What is confession?
Confession consists of two parts. One is that we confess our sins. The other is that we receive the absolution, that is, forgiveness, from the pastor as from God himself and by no means doubt but firmly believe that our sins are thereby forgiven before God in heaven.

Which sins is a person to confess?
Before God one is to acknowledge the guilt for all sins, even those of which we are not aware, as we do in the Lord's Prayer. However, before the pastor we are to confess only those sins of which we have knowledge and which trouble us.

Which sins are these?
Here reflect on your place in life in light of the Ten Commandments: whether you are father, mother, son, daughter, master, mistress, servant; whether you have been disobedient, unfaithful, lazy, whether you have harmed anyone by word or deed; whether you have stolen, neglected, wasted, or injured anything.

THE SACRAMENT OF THE ALTAR

What is the Sacrament of the Altar?
It is the true body and blood of our Lord Jesus Christ under the bread and wine, instituted by Christ himself for us Christians to eat and to drink.

Where is this written?
The holy evangelists Matthew, Mark, and Luke, and St. Paul write thus:

"In the night in which he was betrayed, our Lord Jesus took bread, and gave thanks; broke it, and gave it to his disciples, saying: Take and eat; this is my body, given for you. Do this for the remembrance of me. Again, after supper, he took the cup, gave thanks, and gave it for all to drink, saying: This cup is the new covenant in my blood, shed for you and for all people for the forgiveness of sin. Do this for the remembrance of me."

What is the benefit of such eating and drinking?
The words "given for you" and "shed for you for the forgiveness of sin" show us that forgiveness of sin, life, and salvation are given to us in the sacrament through these words, because where there is forgiveness of sin, there is also life and salvation.

How can bodily eating and drinking do such a great thing?
Eating and drinking certainly do not do it, but rather the words that are recorded: "given for you" and "shed for you for the forgiveness of sin." These words, when accompanied by the physical eating and drinking, are the essential thing in the sacrament, and whoever believes these very words has what they declare and state, namely, "forgiveness of sin."

Who, then, receives this sacrament worthily?
Fasting and bodily preparation are in fact a fine external discipline, but a person who has faith in these words, "given for you" and "shed for you for the forgiveness of sin," is really worthy and well prepared. However, a person who does not believe these words or doubts them is unworthy and unprepared, because the words "for you" require truly believing hearts.

THE MORNING BLESSING

In the morning, as soon as you get out of bed, you are to make the sign of the holy cross and say:
"God the Father, Son, and Holy Spirit watch over me. Amen."

Then, kneeling or standing, say the Apostles' Creed and the Lord's Prayer. If you wish, you may in addition recite this little prayer as well:
"I give thanks to you, heavenly Father, through Jesus Christ your dear Son, that you have protected me through the night from all harm and danger. I ask that you would also protect me today from sin and all evil, so that my life and actions may please you. Into your hands I commend myself: my body, my soul, and all that is mine. Let your holy angel be with me, so that the wicked foe may have no power over me. Amen."

After singing a hymn perhaps (for example, one on the Ten Commandments) or whatever else may serve your devotion, you are to go to your work joyfully.

THE EVENING BLESSING

In the evening, when you go to bed, you are to make the sign of the holy cross and say:
"God the Father, Son, and Holy Spirit watch over me. Amen."

Then, kneeling or standing, say the Apostles' Creed and the Lord's Prayer. If you wish, you may in addition recite this little prayer as well:
"I give thanks to you, heavenly Father, through Jesus Christ your dear Son, that you have graciously protected me today. I ask you to forgive me all my sins, where I have done wrong, and graciously to protect me tonight. Into your hands I commend myself: my body, my soul, and all that is mine. Let your holy angel be with me, so that the wicked foe may have no power over me. Amen."

Then you are to go to sleep quickly and cheerfully.

TABLE BLESSINGS

The children and the members of the household are to come devoutly to the table, fold their hands, and recite: "The eyes of all wait upon you, O Lord, and you give them their food in due season. You open your hand and satisfy the desire of every living creature."

Then they are to recite the Lord's Prayer and the following prayer:
"Lord God, heavenly Father, bless us and these your gifts, which we receive from your bountiful goodness, through Jesus Christ our Lord. Amen."

Similarly, after eating they should in the same manner fold their hands and recite devoutly:
"Give thanks to the Lord, for the Lord is good, for God's mercy endures forever. God provides food for the cattle and for the young ravens when they cry. God is not impressed by the might of a horse, and has no pleasure in the speed of a runner, but finds pleasure in those who fear the Lord, in those who await God's steadfast love."

Then recite the Lord's Prayer and the following prayer:
"We give thanks to you, Lord God our Father, through Jesus Christ our Lord for all your benefits, you who live and reign forever. Amen."

NOTES & STUFF

NOTES & STUFF

NOTES & STUFF

NOTES & STUFF

NOTES & STUFF

NOTES & STUFF

NOTES & STUFF

NOTES & STUFF